KT-382-409

The little TAPAS book

MURDOCH BOOKS

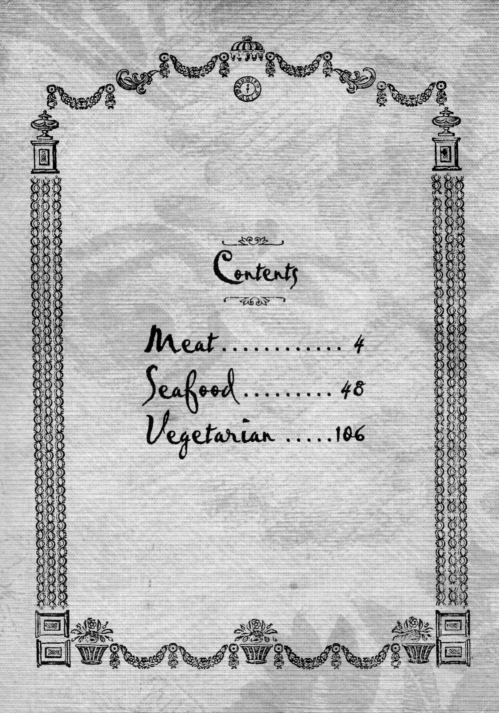

Contents

Meat 4

Seafood 48

Vegetarian 106

Meat

Chorizo in cider

PREPARATION 10 minutes
COOKING 20 minutes   SERVES 4

3 teaspoons olive oil

1 small brown onion, finely chopped

1½ teaspoons sweet paprika (pimentón)

125 ml (4 fl oz/½ cup) sidra (alcoholic apple cider)

60 ml (2 fl oz/¼ cup) chicken stock

1 bay leaf

2 chorizo (approx. 300 g/ 10½ oz in total), sliced diagonally

2 teaspoons sherry vinegar, or to taste

2 teaspoons chopped flat-leaf (Italian) parsley

Heat the oil in a saucepan over low heat, add the onion and cook for 5 minutes, or until soft, stirring occasionally. Add the paprika and cook for 1 minute.

Increase the heat to medium, add the cider, stock and bay leaf to the pan and bring to the boil. Reduce the heat and simmer for 5 minutes. Add the chorizo and simmer for 5 minutes, or until the sauce has reduced slightly. Stir in the sherry vinegar and parsley. Season to taste. Serve hot.

Ham and olive empanadillas

PREPARATION *35 minutes*
COOKING *25 minutes* MAKES *about 15*

2 hard-boiled eggs, roughly
chopped

40 g (1¼ oz/¼ cup) chopped
stuffed green olives

95 g (3 oz) ham, finely
chopped

30 g (1 oz/¼ cup) grated
cheddar

3 sheets ready-rolled puff
pastry

1 egg yolk, lightly beaten

Preheat the oven to hot 220°C (425°F/Gas 7). Lightly grease
two baking trays. Combine the eggs with the olives, ham and
cheddar in a bowl.

Cut puff pastry sheets into 10 cm (4 inch) rounds (about five
rounds from each sheet.) Spoon a tablespoon of the mixture
into the centre of each round, fold over the pastry to enclose
the filling and crimp the edges to seal.

Place the pastries on the trays 2 cm (¾ inch) apart. Brush with
egg yolk and bake for 15 minutes, or until brown and puffed.
Swap trays around after 10 minutes. Cover loosely with foil if
browning too much. Serve hot.

Fried breadcrumbs with eggs

PREPARATION *20 minutes*   COOKING *40 minutes*   SERVES *4*

4 thick slices white bread, crusts removed

2 tablespoons extra virgin olive oil

125 ml (4 fl oz/½ cup) mild olive oil

1 red onion, cut into 2 cm (¾ inch) cubes

2 garlic cloves, crushed

2 red capsicums (peppers), cut into 2 cm (¾ inch) squares

100 g (3½ oz) thinly sliced jamón, cut into fine strips

2 chorizo, cut into 2 cm (¾ inch) cubes

½ teaspoon smoked Spanish paprika

4 eggs

2 tablespoons chopped flat-leaf (Italian) parsley

Cut or tear the bread into small pieces or large crumbs. Heat the extra virgin olive oil in a large heavy-based frying pan over medium heat. Add the bread pieces and toss to coat in the oil then stir continuously for 3–4 minutes or until lightly golden. Remove and drain on paper towel. Season with salt and pepper and allow to cool.

Heat 2 tablespoons of mild olive oil in the same pan used for the bread over medium heat. Add the onion, garlic and red capsicum and stir until softened, for about 10 minutes. Add the jamón, chorizo and paprika and continue to cook on medium heat until lightly browned, another 10 minutes. Sprinkle with half the bread pieces and stir through. Remove from heat and keep warm in a low oven while cooking eggs.

Put the remaining oil in a clean frypan over medium heat. When hot, quickly crack 4 eggs into the oil. Using a metal spoon scoop hot oil from the base of the pan over the eggs so that they become crispy around the edges while yolk remains soft. Remove from oil and drain eggs.

To serve, divide the breadcrumb mixture between 4 serving dishes; top each with a fried egg and sprinkle with parsley.

Jamones
de Salamanca
781 kg.

LATAS
DE CERVEZA
Y REFRESCOS

PTS.	EUROS
	075

QUESOS:
BURGOS
CABRA
VILLALÓN
3,55

14·32

78·13

4·90

4·90

6·30

4·51

Caprichos

Caprichos

Garlic lamb skewers

PREPARATION *15 minutes*
COOKING TIME *5 minutes*   MAKES *35*

600 g (1 lb 5 oz) trimmed
  lamb steaks
1 garlic bulb
1 red chilli, chopped
2 garlic cloves, crushed
60 ml (2 fl oz/¼ cup) oil

Cut the lamb steaks into 2 cm (¾ inch) cubes and halve each
garlic clove lengthways.

Thread 2 pieces of lamb and 2 slices of garlic alternately onto
35 small metal skewers.

Combine chilli, crushed garlic cloves and oil. Heat a chargrill
pan and lightly brush with oil. Cook skewers for 2–5 minutes,
brushing occasionally with garlic and chilli marinade.

Meatballs

PREPARATION 15 minutes + chilling time
COOKING 35 minutes   SERVES 6

175 g (6 oz) minced (ground)
  pork

175 g (6 oz) minced (ground)
  veal

3 garlic cloves, crushed

35 g (1¼ oz/⅓ cup) dry
  breadcrumbs

1 teaspoon ground coriander

1 teaspoon ground nutmeg

1 teaspoon ground cumin

pinch of ground cinnamon

1 egg

2 tablespoons olive oil

Spicy tomato sauce

1 tablespoon olive oil

1 brown onion, chopped

2 garlic cloves, crushed

125 ml (4 fl oz/½ cup) dry
  white wine

400 g (14 oz) tinned chopped
  tomatoes

1 tablespoon tomato paste
  (concentrated purée)

125 ml (4 fl oz/½ cup)
  chicken stock

½ teaspoon cayenne pepper

80 g (2¾ oz/½ cup) frozen
  peas

Combine the pork, veal, garlic, breadcrumbs, spices, egg and
season with salt and pepper in a bowl. Mix by hand until the
mixture is smooth and leaves the side of the bowl. Refrigerate,
covered, for 30 minutes.

Roll tablespoons of the mixture into balls. Heat 1 tablespoon
of olive oil in a frying pan and toss half the meatballs over
medium—high heat for about 2—3 minutes, or until browned.
Drain on paper towel. Add remaining oil, if necessary, and
brown the rest of the meatballs. Drain on paper towel.

To make the sauce, heat the oil in a frying pan over medium
heat and cook the onion, stirring occasionally, for 3 minutes,
or until translucent. Add the garlic and cook for 1 minute.
Increase the heat to high, add the wine and boil for 1 minute.
Add the chopped tomatoes, the tomato paste and stock and
simmer for 10 minutes. Stir in the cayenne pepper, peas and
the meatballs and simmer for 5—10 minutes, or until sauce is
thick. Serve hot.

The little TAPAS book

Plaza Toros de COLLADO VILLA

Empresa: EXCMO. AYUNTAMIENTO - Organiza: COMISION DE MAYORDOMOS Y TOMAS ENTERO, S.L. - Co

5 SENSAC
ACONTECI
TAURIN

NOVILLADA SIN PICADORES	VIERNES 15 7 TARDE	NOVILLADA SIN
6 HERMOSOS NOVILLOS Toros de Triana		6 HERMOSOS NOVILLOS
...LOS GUARD 5 (Sevilla) para los valientes novilleros ESPADAS		de COLMENAREJO (Madrid) para los valie
RONIMO MIGUEL PABLO ELGADO - NAVARRO - LECHUGA	JUAN CARLOS TOMAS REY - CERQUEIRA

Chilli beef quesadillas

PREPARATION **15 minutes**   COOKING **25 minutes**   MAKES **about 36**

1½ tablespoons oil

1 onion, chopped

2 garlic cloves, crushed

400 g (14 oz) minced (ground) beef

325 g (11 oz) ready-made Mexican black bean salsa

6 flour tortillas

125 g (4½ oz/1 cup) grated cheddar

Heat 1 tablespoon of the oil in a frying pan and cook onion and garlic for 2–3 minutes. Add the beef and cook for about 5–7 minutes, or until brown, breaking up any lumps. Stir in the salsa. Bring to the boil, reduce the heat and simmer for 3–4 minutes, or until mixture reduces and thickens. Season.

Put three of the tortillas on a work surface and sprinkle with the cheddar. Spoon the beef evenly over the cheese, then top with another three tortillas. Heat the remaining oil in a 25 cm (10 inch) frying pan and cook the stacks for 3–4 minutes each side, or until golden brown. Remove from the pan, trim off the sides and cut into 5 cm (2 inch) squares.

Arancini

PREPARATION 20 minutes + chilling time
COOKING 40 minutes MAKES 10

440 g (15½ oz/2 cups) risotto rice

1 egg, lightly beaten

1 egg yolk

50 g (¾ oz/1 cup) grated parmesan

plain (all-purpose) flour, to coat

2 eggs, lightly beaten

dry breadcrumbs, to coat

oil, for deep-frying

Meat sauce

1 dried porcini mushroom

1 tablespoon olive oil

1 onion, chopped

125 g (4½ oz) minced beef or veal

2 slices prosciutto, chopped

2 tablespoons tomato paste

80 ml (2½ fl oz/⅓ cup) white wine

½ teaspoon dried thyme leaves

3 tablespoons fresh parsley

Cook the rice in boiling water for 20 minutes, or until just soft. Drain, without rinsing, and cool. Put in a large bowl and add the egg, egg yolk and parmesan. Stir until the rice sticks together. Cover and set aside.

To make the meat sauce, soak the mushroom in hot water for 10 minutes to soften, then squeeze dry and chop finely. Heat oil in a frying pan. Add mushroom and onion and cook for 3 minutes, or until soft. Add mince and cook, stirring, until browned. Add the prosciutto, tomato paste, wine, thyme and pepper to taste. Cook, stirring, for 5 minutes, or until all the liquid is absorbed. Stir in the parsley and set aside to cool.

With wet hands, form the rice mixture into 10 balls. Wet your hands again and gently pull the balls apart. Place 3 teaspoons of the meat sauce in the centre of each. Reshape to enclose the filling. Roll in the flour, beaten egg and breadcrumbs and chill for 1 hour.

Fill a deep heavy-based pan one-third full of oil and heat to 180°C (350°F), or until a cube of bread browns in 15 seconds. Deep-fry croquettes, two at a time, for 3–4 minutes, or until golden brown. Drain on paper towels and keep warm while cooking the rest.

Kibbeh

PREPARATION *25 minutes + chilling time*
COOKING *25 minutes* MAKES *15*

235 g (8½ oz/1⅓ cups)
fine burghul (bulgur)

150 g (5½ oz) lean lamb,
chopped

1 onion, grated

2 tablespoons plain
(all-purpose) flour

1 teaspoon ground allspice

Filling

2 teaspoons olive oil

1 small onion, finely chopped

100 g (3½ oz) lean minced
(ground) lamb

½ teaspoon ground allspice

½ teaspoon ground cinnamon

80 ml (2½ fl oz/⅓ cup) beef
stock

2 tablespoons pine nuts

2 tablespoons chopped mint

Put the burghul in a large bowl, cover with boiling water and leave for 5 minutes. Drain in a colander, pressing well to remove the water. Spread on paper towels to absorb the remaining moisture.

Process the burghul, lamb, onion, flour and allspice until a fine paste forms. Season well, then refrigerate for 1 hour.

To make filling, heat the oil in a frying pan, add onion and cook over low heat for 3 minutes, or until soft. Add the lamb, allspice and cinnamon, and stir over high heat for 3 minutes. Add the stock and cook, partially covered, over low heat for 6 minutes, or until lamb is soft. Roughly chop the pine nuts and stir in with the mint. Season, then transfer to a bowl and allow to cool.

Shape 2 tablespoons of the burghul mixture into a sausage shape 6 cm (2½ inches) long. Dip your hands in cold water and, with your finger, make a long hole through the centre and gently work your finger around to make a shell. Fill with 2 teaspoons of the filling and seal, moulding it into a torpedo shape. Smooth over any cracks with your fingers. Put on a foil-lined tray and repeat with the remaining ingredients to make 15 kibbeh. Refrigerate, uncovered, for 1 hour.

Fill a deep heavy-based frying pan one-third full of oil and heat oil to 180°C (350°F), or until a cube of bread dropped into the oil turns golden brown in 15 seconds. Deep-fry the kibbeh in batches for 2–3 minutes, or until well browned. Drain on crumpled paper towels.

Chorizo and tomato salsa

PREPARATION 15 minutes
COOKING 20 minutes MAKES 3 cups

2 tablespoons olive oil

250 g (9 oz) chorizo sausage, finely chopped

4 garlic cloves, finely chopped

4 small celery sticks, finely chopped

2 bay leaves

1 red onion, finely chopped

2 teaspoons sweet paprika

6 ripe tomatoes, peeled, seeded, chopped

2 tablespoons tomato paste (purée)

2 x 130 g (4½ oz) cans corn kernels, drained

50 g (¾ oz/1 cup) roughly chopped fresh coriander (cilantro) leaves

1 tablespoon sugar

Heat oil in a large frying pan. Add the sausage, garlic, celery, bay leaves, onion and paprika. Cook, stirring, over medium heat for 10 minutes.

Add tomato, tomato paste and corn and cook over high heat for 5 minutes, or until tomato is pulpy and mixture is thick.

Remove the pan from the heat, stir through the coriander and sugar and season. Serve hot.

Cordoban pork rolls

PREPARATION *25 minutes + chilling time*
COOKING *35 minutes* SERVES *4-6*

100 g (3½ oz) butter

60 g (2¼ oz/½ cup) plain (all-purpose) flour

185 ml (6 fl oz/¾ cup) milk

185 ml (6 fl oz/¾ cup) chicken stock

4 pork schnitzel pieces, 100 g (3½ oz) each

4 thin slices jamón, 100 g (3½ oz) each

2 tablespoons chopped flat-leaf (Italian) parsley

2 garlic cloves, finely chopped

2 large eggs

dash of milk

plain (all-purpose) flour, for coating

dried breadcrumbs, for coating

olive oil, for deep-frying

In a saucepan, melt the butter over low–medium heat. Add the flour and cook for 1–2 minutes, stirring. Slowly whisk in the combined milk and stock mixture. Season and then stir for 8–10 minutes, or until quite thick. Cool to room temperature, then cover and refrigerate until well chilled.

Using a mallet, pound the pork until about 5 mm thick and slightly longer and wider than the jamón slices. Trim edges to form neat rectangles.

Lay a piece of jamón over the top of each rectangle. Combine the parsley and garlic and sprinkle on top. Roll up and hold in place with a toothpick. Refrigerate until ready to use.

When white sauce is cold and firm remove from refrigerator. You will need to mould the sauce around the pork. Add a little milk if mix is too thick and won't stick to the pork. Note that the mixture just needs to coat the pork – work quickly, it doesn't need to look too neat as the pork will be coated in crumbs. Place on a tray in a single layer, cover and refrigerate for 1 hour to firm up again.

Place the eggs and a dash of milk in a bowl and combine. Place the flour and breadcrumbs on separate plates. Lightly coat the pork rolls in the flour then dip into the egg wash, then lift out allowing any excess to drip off then roll in the breadcrumbs. Continue until all are coated. Refrigerate until ready to cook to firm crumbs. Preheat the oven to 180°C (350°F/Gas 4).

Meanwhile fill a deep-fryer or a heavy-based casserole dish one-third full of oil and heat the oil to 180°C (350°F). Fry the pork until golden, about 1 minute on each side. Place in the oven for 15–20 minutes, or until firm to touch. Remove toothpicks and serve.

Croquettes

PREPARATION 20 minutes + chilling time
COOKING 30 minutes MAKES 24

90 g (3¼ oz/⅓ cup) butter

1 small brown onion, finely chopped

115 g (4 oz) open cap mushrooms, finely chopped

125 g (4½ oz/1 cup) plain (all-purpose) flour

250 ml (9 fl oz/1 cup) milk

185 ml (6 fl oz/¾ cup) chicken stock

115 g (4 oz) jamón or prosciutto, finely chopped

60 g (2¼ oz/½ cup) plain (all-purpose) flour, extra

2 eggs, lightly beaten

50 g (1¾ oz/½ cup) dry breadcrumbs

olive oil, for deep-frying

Melt the butter in a saucepan over low heat, add the onion and cook for 5 minutes, or until translucent. Add the mushrooms and cook over low heat, stirring occasionally, for 5 minutes. Add the flour and stir over low–medium heat for 1 minute, or until the mixture is dry and crumbly and begins to change colour. Remove from the heat and gradually add the milk, stirring until smooth. Stir in the stock and return to the heat, stirring until the mixture boils and thickens. Stir in the jamón and some black pepper, then transfer the mixture to a bowl to cool for about 2 hours.

Roll heaped tablespoons of the mixture into croquette shapes about 6 cm (2½ inch) long. Put the extra flour, beaten egg and breadcrumbs in three separate shallow bowls. Toss the croquettes in the flour, dip in the egg, allowing the excess to drain away, then roll in the breadcrumbs. Put on a baking tray and refrigerate for about 30 minutes.

Fill a deep, heavy-based saucepan one-third full of oil and heat to 170°C (325°F), or until a cube of bread dropped into the oil browns in 20 seconds. Add the croquettes in batches and deep-fry for 3 minutes, turning, until brown. Drain well on paper towel. Sprinkle with salt before serving hot.

Mushroom and prosciutto skewers

PREPARATION *10 minutes* COOKING *10 minutes* MAKES *24*

48 cremini mushrooms

90 g (3¼ oz/⅓ cup) butter

125 ml (4 fl oz/½ cup) port

18 slices of prosciutto, each cut into 4 pieces

Wipe the mushrooms with a damp cloth, then cut them in half. Melt the butter in a frying pan and add the mushrooms and a pinch of salt. Cook, stirring, over medium heat for 1 minute. Add the port and cook, stirring, until it evaporates completely. Remove from the heat.

Thread four pieces of mushroom and three rolled pieces of prosciutto alternately onto wooden skewers and serve.

Broad beans with jamón

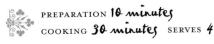

PREPARATION 10 minutes
COOKING 30 minutes SERVES 4

20 g (¾ oz) butter

1 brown onion, chopped

175 g (6 oz) jamón or
 prosciutto, roughly
 chopped

2 garlic cloves, crushed

500 g (1 lb 2 oz) broad (fava)
 beans, fresh or frozen

125 ml (4 fl oz/½ cup) dry
 white wine

185 ml (6 fl oz/¾ cup)
 chicken stock

Melt the butter in a large saucepan and add the onion, jamón
and garlic. Cook over medium heat for 5 minutes, stirring
often, until the onion softens.

Add the broad beans and wine and cook over high heat until
the liquid is reduced by half. Add the stock, reduce the heat
to low—medium, cover and cook for 10 minutes. Uncover and
simmer for another 10 minutes or until the broad beans are
tender and most of the liquid has evaporated. Serve hot as a
tapas dish with crusty bread, or as a side dish.

Lamb and filo cigars

PREPARATION 30 minutes COOKING 25 minutes MAKES 12

1 tablespoon olive oil

1 small brown onion, finely chopped

350 g (12 oz) lean minced (ground) lamb

2 garlic cloves, crushed

2 teaspoons ground cumin

½ teaspoon ground ginger

½ teaspoon paprika

½ teaspoon ground cinnamon

pinch of saffron threads, soaked in a little warm water

2 tablespoons chopped coriander (cilantro) leaves

2 tablespoons chopped flat-leaf (Italian) parsley

1 egg

8–12 sheets filo pastry

90 g (3¼ oz/⅓ cup) butter, melted

1 tablespoon sesame seeds

Heat the oil in a large frying pan, add the onion and cook over low heat for 5 minutes, or until the onion is soft. Increase the heat, add the lamb and garlic and cook for 5 minutes, breaking up any lumps with the back of a wooden spoon. Add the spices, chopped coriander and parsley. Season to taste and then cook for 1 minute, stirring to combine.

Transfer the lamb mixture to a sieve and drain to remove the fat. Put the mixture in a bowl and allow to cool slightly. Mix in the egg.

Count out eight sheets of filo pastry. Stack on a cutting surface with longer side in front of you. Measure and mark pastry into three equal strips and cut through the stack with a sharp knife to give strips 12.5–14 cm (5–5½ inches) wide and 28 30 cm (11¼–12 inches) long. Stack strips in the folds of a dry cloth. (Use extra sheets if pastry is less than 38 cm (15 inches) long.)

Place a strip of filo on the work surface with the narrow end towards you and brush with warm, melted butter. Top with another strip. Place 1 tablespoon of the filling 1 cm (½ inch) in from the base and sides of the strip. Fold the end of the filo over the filling, fold in the sides and roll to the end of the strip. Place on a greased baking tray, seam side down. Repeat with the remaining ingredients. Brush the rolls with melted butter and sprinkle with sesame seeds.

Preheat the oven to 180°C (350°F/Gas 4). It is best to do this after the rolls are completed so that the kitchen remains cool during shaping. Bake the briouats for 15 minutes, or until lightly golden. Serve hot.

Little sandwiches

PREPARATION 10 minutes
MAKES 6

6 mini crispy bread rolls

90 ml (3 fl oz) allioli (see page 111) or ready-made garlic mayonnaise or sauce

12 slices jamón or prosciutto

300 g (10½ oz) pimiento de picillo, cut into strips

150 g (5½ oz) Manchego cheese, thinly sliced

Cut open the bread rolls with a bread knife, leaving them hinged, then spread with the garlic mayonnaise or sauce.

Put two slices of jamón on top of the mayonnaise or sauce, followed by some strips of pimiento and slices of Manchego. Serve immediately.

Seafood

Fried pastries with seafood

PREPARATION **25 minutes** COOKING **15 minutes** MAKES **24**

Fish or prawn filling

250 g (9 oz) boneless white fish fillets, or 200 g (7 oz) cooked prawns (shrimp), peeled and deveined

2 tablespoons finely chopped flat-leaf (Italian) parsley

1 tablespoon spring onion (scallion), finely chopped

1 garlic clove, crushed

½ teaspoon paprika

¼ teaspoon ground cumin

pinch of cayenne pepper

1 tablespoon lemon juice

1 tablespoon olive oil

6 sheets filo pastry

1 egg white, lightly beaten

oil, for deep-frying

3 tablespoons caster (superfine) sugar, to serve

⅛ teaspoon cayenne pepper, to serve

1 teaspoon ground cinnamon, to serve

To make the fish or prawn filling, first poach the fish gently in lightly salted water, to cover, until the flesh flakes — about 4–5 minutes. Remove from the poaching liquid to a plate and cover closely with plastic wrap so that the surface does not dry as it cools. When cool, flake the fish and put it in a bowl. If using cooked prawns, cut them into small pieces. Put the fish or the prawns in a bowl, add the parsley, spring onion, garlic, paprika, cumin, cayenne pepper, lemon juice and olive oil and toss well to mix.

Stack filo sheets on a cutting board, and with a ruler and sharp knife, measure and cut across the width of the pastry to give strips 12 cm (4½ inch) wide and 28–30 cm (11¼–12 inch) long. Stack the cut filo in the folds of a dry tea towel (dish towel) or cover with plastic wrap to prevent it from drying out.

Take a filo strip and, with the narrow end towards you, fold it in half across its width to make a strip 6 cm (2½ inch) wide. Place a generous teaspoon of filling 2 cm (¾ inch) in from the base of the strip, fold the end diagonally across the filling so that the base lines up with the side of the strip, forming a triangle. Fold straight up once, then fold diagonally to the opposite side. Continue folding until near the end of the strip, then brush the filo lightly with egg white and complete the fold. Place on a cloth-covered tray, seam side down. Cover with a tea towel until ready to fry, and cook within 10 minutes.

Heat oil to 180°C (350°F), or until a cube of bread dropped into the oil browns in 15 seconds. Add four pastries at a time and fry until golden, turning to brown evenly. Remove with a slotted spoon; drain on paper towel. Serve hot with a small bowl of sugar mixed with cayenne and cinnamon.

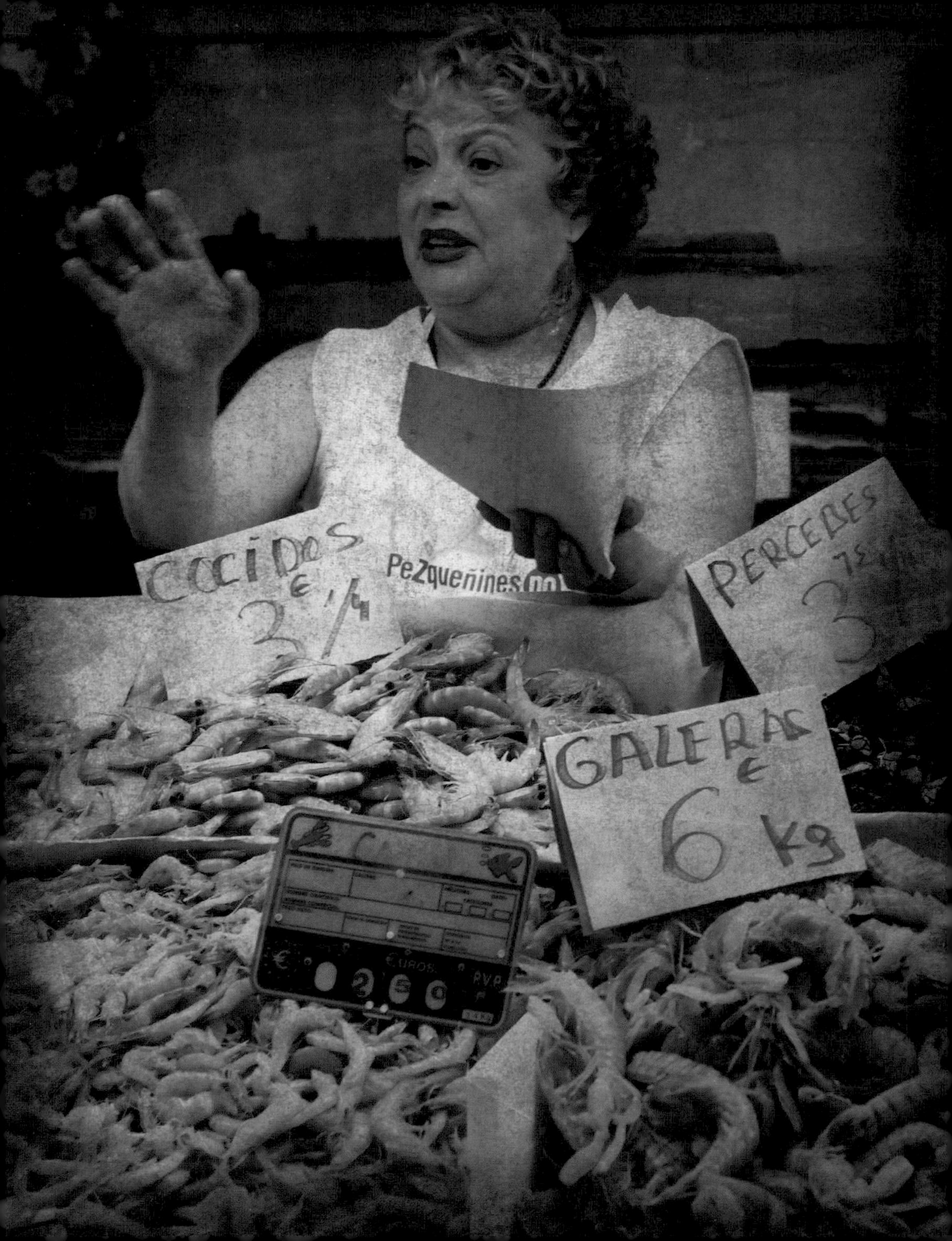
COCIDOS
PeZqueñines
PERCEBES
GALERAS
€
6 Kg

Prawn fritters

PREPARATION 20 minutes + resting time
COOKING 15 minutes MAKES 24 fritters

60 g (2¼ oz/½ cup) plain
(all-purpose) flour, sifted

55 g (2 oz/½ cup) besan
(chickpea flour), sifted

1 teaspoon sweet paprika
(pimentón)

4 large eggs, lightly beaten

4 spring onions (scallions),
finely chopped

1 large handful finely
chopped flat-leaf (Italian)
parsley

500 g (1 lb 2 oz) peeled and
finely chopped raw prawns
(shrimp), about 800 g
(1 lb 12 oz) unpeeled

125 ml (4 fl oz/½ cup) olive
oil

lemon wedges, to serve

Combine flours in a bowl with paprika and make a well in the
centre. Pour in the beaten egg and mix in gradually, then stir
in 60 ml (2 fl oz/¼ cup) water to make a smooth batter. Add
the spring onion, parsley and prawns and season well. Rest the
batter for at least 30 minutes.

Heat oil in a deep-sided frying pan over low–medium heat.
Working in batches, spoon in ½ tablespoons of batter per
fritter and flatten into a thin pancake. Cook for 2–3 minutes
each side, or until golden and cooked through. Remove from
pan and drain on paper towel. Repeat with remaining batter
to make 24 fritters. Season well and serve with lemon wedges.

Pan-fried calamari

PREPARATION 15 minutes + chilling time
COOKING 10 minutes SERVES 4

500 g (1 lb 2 oz) small squid
2 tablespoons olive oil

Picada

2 tablespoons extra virgin
olive oil

2 tablespoons finely chopped
flat-leaf (Italian) parsley

1 garlic clove, crushed

To clean squid, gently pull tentacles away from tube (intestines should come away at the same time). Remove intestines from tentacles by cutting under eyes, then remove beak if it remains in centre of tentacles by using your fingers to push up the centre. Pull away soft bone from hood.

Rub tubes under cold running water. The skin should come away easily. Wash hoods and tentacles and drain well. Transfer to a bowl, add ¼ teaspoon salt and mix well. Cover and then refrigerate for 30 minutes. Close to serving time, whisk picada ingredients in a bowl with ¼ teaspoon black pepper and salt.

Heat oil in a frying pan over high heat and cook squid hoods in small batches for 2–3 minutes, or until they turn white. Cook tentacles, turning to brown them all over, for 1 minute, or until they curl up. Drizzle with the picada and serve hot.

Whitebait fritters with tartare sauce

PREPARATION 20 minutes + chilling time
COOKING 10 minutes MAKES 50

125 g (¼ oz/1 cup) plain (all-purpose) flour

1 large egg, lightly beaten

250 ml (9 fl oz/1 cup) iced water

3 tablespoons chopped fresh parsley

3 teaspoons grated lemon zest

400 g (14 oz) whitebait

oil, for deep-frying

Tartare sauce

2 egg yolks

1 teaspoon Dijon mustard

250 ml (9 fl oz/1 cup) olive oil

1 tablespoon lemon juice

2 tablespoons capers

2 tablespoons gherkins

1 tablespoon parsley

1 tablespoon tarragon

Sift the flour and a pinch of salt and pepper into a large bowl, make a well in the centre and add the egg. Whisk gently and gradually add water, stirring constantly to a smooth batter. Stir in parsley and lemon zest. Refrigerate, covered, for 1 hour.

To make the tartare sauce, drain the capers and then chop the capers, gherkins, parsley and tarragon. Place the egg yolks and mustard in a food processor and pulse for 10 seconds. With the motor running, slowly add the oil in a thin stream until the mixture is thick and creamy. Add lemon juice and 2 teaspoons boiling water and pulse for another 10 seconds. Transfer to a bowl, add capers, gherkins, parsley and tarragon and season generously. Cover and refrigerate until needed.

Pat the whitebait dry, then gently stir into the batter. Fill a large heavy-based saucepan one-third full of oil and heat to 190°C (375°F), or until a cube of bread dropped in the oil browns in 10 seconds. Put small tablespoons of batter into the oil. Cook the fritters in batches, gently tossing in the oil. Cook for 2 minutes, or until the fritters are golden brown. Drain on crumpled paper towels and keep warm. Repeat with remaining mixture. Serve immediately with the tartare sauce.

Tuna skewers

PREPARATION *20 minutes + soaking time*
COOKING *5 minutes* MAKES *8*

250 g (9 oz) raw tuna

1 lemon

1 tablespoon lemon juice

1 tablespoon extra virgin olive
   oil

16 caper berries

8 green olives, stuffed with
   anchovies

Soak eight wooden skewers in cold water for 1 hour to prevent
them burning during cooking. Cut tuna into 24 even-sized
cubes. Remove the zest from the lemon, avoiding the bitter
white pith, and cut the zest into thin strips.

Combine the tuna, the lemon zest, the lemon juice and the
olive oil in a bowl.

Thread three pieces of tuna, two caper berries and one green
olive onto each skewer, alternating each ingredient. Put in a
non-metallic dish and pour marinade over them. Cook under
a hot grill (broiler), turning to cook each side, for 4 minutes,
or until done to your liking.

Fish and cumin kebabs

PREPARATION **10 minutes** COOKING **10 minutes** SERVES **4**

750 g (1 lb 10 oz) skinless
firm white fish fillets, such
as blue-eye, snapper or
perch

2 tablespoons olive oil

1 garlic clove, crushed

3 tablespoons chopped
coriander (cilantro) leaves

2 teaspoons ground cumin

Cut the fish fillets into 3 cm (1¼ inch) cubes. Thread on oiled
skewers and set aside.

To make marinade, combine the oil, garlic, coriander, cumin
and 1 teaspoon ground black pepper in a small bowl. Brush the
marinade over the fish, cover with plastic wrap and refrigerate
for several hours, or overnight, turning occasionally. Drain,
reserving the marinade. Season just before cooking.

Put the skewers on a hot, lightly oiled barbecue flatplate. Cook
for 5–6 minutes, or until tender, turning once and brushing
with reserved marinade several times during cooking.

Garlic prawns

PREPARATION *20 minutes*
COOKING *20 minutes* SERVES *4*

1¼ kg (2 lb 12 oz) raw prawns
  (shrimp)

80 g (2¾ oz) butter, melted

185 ml (6 fl oz/¾ cups) olive
  oil

8 garlic cloves, crushed

2 spring onions (scallions),
  thinly sliced

crusty bread, to serve

Preheat the oven to 250°C (500°F/Gas 9). Peel the prawns, leaving tails intact. Pull out the vein from the back, starting at the head end. Cut a slit down the back of each prawn.

Combine the butter and oil and divide among four 500 ml (17 fl oz/2 cups) cast-iron pots. Divide half the crushed garlic among the pots.

Place the pots on a baking tray and heat in the oven for 10 minutes, or until the mixture is bubbling. Remove from the oven and divide prawns and remaining garlic among the pots. Return to the oven for 5 minutes, or until the prawns are cooked. Stir in the spring onion. Season to taste. Serve with bread to mop up the juices.

Russian salad

PREPARATION *20 minutes*
COOKING *25 minutes* SERVES *4-6*

Mayonnaise

2 egg yolks

1 teaspoon dijon mustard

125 ml (4 fl oz/½ cup) extra
   virgin olive oil

2 tablespoons lemon juice

2 small garlic cloves, crushed

3 bottled artichoke hearts

3 all-purpose potatoes, such
   as desiree, unpeeled

100 g (3½ oz) baby green
   beans, trimmed and cut
   into 1 cm (½ inch) lengths

1 large carrot, cut into 1 cm
   (½ inch) dice

125 g (4½ oz) fresh peas

30 g (1 oz) cornichons,
   chopped

2 tablespoons baby capers,
   rinsed and drained

4 anchovy fillets, finely
   chopped

10 black olives, each cut into
   3 slices

whole black olives, extra,
   to garnish

To make mayonnaise, use electric beaters to beat the egg yolks with the mustard and ¼ teaspoon salt until creamy. Gradually add the oil in a fine stream, beating constantly until all the oil has been added. Add lemon juice, garlic and 1 teaspoon boiling water and beat for 1 minute, or until well combined. Season to taste.

Cut each artichoke into quarters. Rinse the potatoes, cover with salted cold water and bring to a gentle simmer. Cook for 15–20 minutes, or until tender when pierced with a knife. Drain and allow to cool slightly. Peel and set aside. When the potatoes are completely cool, cut into 1 cm (½ inch) dice.

Blanch the beans in salted boiling water until tender but still firm to the bite. Refresh in cold water, then drain thoroughly. Repeat with the carrot and peas.

Set aside a small quantity of each vegetable, including the cornichons, for the garnish and then season to taste. Put the remainder in a bowl along with capers, anchovies and sliced olives. Add mayonnaise, toss to combine and season. Arrange on a serving dish and garnish with the reserved vegetables and the whole olives.

Stuffed mussels

PREPARATION 20 minutes   TOTAL COOKING 20 minutes   MAKES 18

18 black mussels

2 teaspoons olive oil

2 spring onions (scallions),
   finely chopped

1 garlic clove, crushed

1 tablespoon tomato paste
   (concentrated purée)

2 teaspoons lemon juice

1 large handful flat-leaf
   (Italian) parsley, chopped

75 g (2¾ oz/¾ cup) dry
   breadcrumbs

2 eggs, beaten

olive oil, for deep-frying

White sauce

20 g (¾ oz) butter

1½ tablespoons plain
   (all-purpose) flour

2 tablespoons milk

Scrub the mussels and remove the hairy beards. Discard any open mussels or those that don't close when tapped on the bench. Bring 250 ml (9 fl oz/1 cup) water to the boil in a saucepan, add mussels, then cover and cook for 3–4 minutes, shaking the pan occasionally, until the mussels have opened. Remove them as soon as they open or they will be tough. Strain cooking liquid into a pitcher until you have around 80 ml (2½ fl oz/⅓ cup). Discard any unopened mussels. Remove the rest of the mussels from their shells and discard one half shell from each. Finely chop the mussel meat.

Heat the oil in a frying pan, add the spring onion and cook for 1 minute. Add garlic and cook for 1 minute. Stir in the mussel meat, tomato paste, lemon juice, 2 tablespoons of the parsley and season with salt and pepper. Set aside to cool.

To make the white sauce, melt the butter in a saucepan over low heat. Stir in flour and cook for 1 minute, or until pale and foaming. Remove from heat and gradually whisk in the reserved mussel liquid, the milk and some pepper. Return to heat and cook, stirring, for 1 minute, or until sauce boils and thickens. Reduce heat and simmer for 2 minutes until quite thick. Cool.

Spoon the mussel mixture into the shells. Top each generously with the white sauce and smooth the surface, to form a mound.

Combine the breadcrumbs and the remaining parsley. Dip the mussels in egg, then press in the crumbs to cover the top. Fill a deep, heavy-based saucepan one-third full of oil and heat to 180°C (350°F), or until a cube of bread browns in 15 seconds. Cook the mussels in batches for 10–15 seconds, or until lightly browned. Remove with a slotted spoon and then drain well. Serve hot.

Tuna empanadas

PREPARATION *30 minutes + chilling time*
COOKING *45 minutes* MAKES *24*

400 g (14 oz/3¼ cups) plain (all-purpose) flour, plus extra for rolling

75 g (2¾ oz) butter, softened

2 eggs

60 ml (2 fl oz/¼ cup) fine sherry

1 egg, extra, lightly beaten

Filling

1 tablespoon olive oil

1 small brown onion, finely diced

2 teaspoons tomato paste (concentrated purée)

125 g (4½ oz/½ cup) tinned chopped tomatoes

85 g (3 oz) tinned tuna, drained

1½ tablespoons chopped roasted red capsicum (pepper) (see page 126)

2 tablespoons chopped flat-leaf (Italian) parsley

Sift flour and 1 teaspoon of salt into a large bowl. Rub butter into the flour until the mixture resembles fine breadcrumbs. Combine the eggs and sherry and add to the bowl, cutting the liquid in with a flat-bladed knife until the mixture clumps and forms a dough. Turn onto a lightly floured surface and gather together into a smooth ball (do not knead or the pastry will be tough). Cover with plastic wrap. Refrigerate for 30 minutes.

To make filling, heat the olive oil in a frying pan over medium heat and cook the onion for about 5 minutes, or until softened and translucent. Add tomato paste and chopped tomato and then cook for 10 minutes, or until pulpy. Add tuna, roasted capsicum and parsley and season well.

Preheat oven to 190°C (375°F/Gas 5). Dust a work surface with the extra flour. Roll out half the pastry to a thickness of 2 mm (1/16 inch). Using a 10 cm (4 inch) cutter, cut pastry into 12 rounds. Put a heaped tablespoon of filling on each round, fold over and brush edges with water, then pinch to seal. Continue with the remaining rounds, then repeat with the rest of the dough and filling to make 24 empanadas.

Transfer to a lightly oiled baking tray and then brush each empanada with the extra beaten egg. Bake for 30 minutes, or until golden. Serve warm or cold.

Grilled prawns with tequila mayonnaise

 PREPARATION 10 minutes + chilling time
COOKING 5 minutes MAKES 24

24 raw king prawns

80 ml (2½ fl oz/⅓ cup)
olive oil

2 tablespoons lime juice

1 tablespoon tequila

160 g (5¾ oz/⅔ cup)
whole-egg mayonnaise

Peel and devein the prawns, keeping the tails intact. Combine
the olive oil with the lime juice in a non-metallic bowl and
season with salt and cracked black pepper. Add the prawns,
cover and leave to marinate for 1 hour. Meanwhile, mix the
tequila into the mayonnaise, then transfer to a serving dish.

Heat a barbecue or chargrill pan to hot, add the prawns and
cook for 1–2 minutes on each side until pink and cooked
through. Serve with the tequila mayonnaise for dipping.

Notes: The prawns can be grilled up to an hour beforehand.
One way to save time is to buy pre-cooked prawns from your
fishmonger. Then all you need to do is to peel them, leaving
the tails intact. Squeeze them with lime juice and serve with the
mayonnaise. If you prefer a dipping sauce without alcohol, add
2 tablespoons of chopped fresh herbs, such as dill, basil
or parsley to the mayonnaise instead of tequila.

Scallop fritters

 PREPARATION 20 minutes
COOKING 20 minutes MAKES 40

250 g (9 oz) scallops

6 eggs

25 g (1 oz) parmesan cheese, grated

3 garlic cloves, crushed

125 g (4½ oz/1 cup) plain (all-purpose) flour

2 tablespoons chopped thyme

2 tablespoons oregano, chopped

oil, for pan-frying

whole-egg mayonnaise, to serve

Clean and roughly chop the scallops. Lightly beat eggs and combine with the parmesan, the garlic, the flour and the herbs. Stir in scallops.

Heat 3 cm (1¼ inch) oil in a deep frying pan to 180°C (350°F), or until a cube of bread dropped into the oil turns golden brown in 15 seconds. Cook fritters in batches. Using 1 tablespoon of batter for each fritter, pour into oil and cook for 4–5 minutes, until golden brown. Drain on crumpled paper towels and then sprinkle lightly with salt. Serve with mayonnaise for dipping.

Saffron fish balls in tomato sauce

PREPARATION *20 minutes*
COOKING *45 minutes*   SERVES *4*

500 g (1 lb 2 oz) boneless
   firm white fish fillets

1 egg

2 spring onions (scallions),
   chopped

1 tablespoon chopped
   flat-leaf (Italian) parsley

1 tablespoon chopped
   coriander (cilantro) leaves

55 g (2 oz/²/₃ cup) fresh
   breadcrumbs

small pinch saffron threads

Tomato sauce

500 g (1 lb 2 oz) tomatoes

1 brown onion, coarsely
   grated

3 tablespoons olive oil

2 garlic cloves, finely
   chopped

1 teaspoon paprika

½ teaspoon harissa, or
   to taste, or ¼ teaspoon
   cayenne pepper

½ teaspoon ground cumin

1 teaspoon caster (superfine)
   sugar

Cut the fish fillets into rough pieces and put in a food processor bowl, along with the egg, spring onion, parsley, coriander and breadcrumbs. Soak saffron in 1 tablespoon warm water for 5 minutes and add to other ingredients with ¾ teaspoon salt and some freshly ground black pepper. Process to a thick paste, scraping down the sides of the bowl every now and then.

With moistened hands, shape fish mixture into balls the size of a walnut. Put on a tray, cover and set aside in the refrigerator.

To make the tomato sauce, first peel the tomatoes by scoring a cross in the base of each one. Put them in a bowl of boiling water for 20 seconds, then plunge into a bowl of cold water to cool. Remove from the water and peel the skin away from the cross — it should slip off easily. Halve the tomatoes crossways and squeeze out the seeds. Chop the tomatoes and set aside.

Put onion and olive oil in a saucepan and cook over medium heat for 5 minutes. Add the garlic, the paprika, harissa and cumin. Stir for a few seconds, then add the tomato, the sugar, 250 ml (9 fl oz/1 cup) water, and salt and freshly ground black pepper, to taste. Bring to the boil, cover, reduce heat and then simmer for 15 minutes.

Add fish balls to the tomato sauce, shaking the pan occasionally as they are added so that they settle into the sauce. Return to a gentle boil over medium heat, then cover and reduce the heat to low. Simmer for 20 minutes. Serve hot with crusty bread.

The little TAPAS book

Oysters and lemon herb dressing

PREPARATION 10 minutes MAKES 24

24 fresh oysters on the half shell

1 tablespoon dill, chopped

1 garlic clove, crushed

1 tablespoon finely chopped flat-leaf (Italian) parsley

2 teaspoons finely chopped chives

2 tablespoons lemon juice

3 tablespoons extra virgin olive oil

brown bread, cut into small cubes, to serve

Remove the oysters from their shells. Wash the shells in hot water and pat dry. Replace the oysters and cover with a damp cloth in the refrigerator.

Put the dill, garlic, parsley, chives, lemon juice and oil in a bowl and season to taste with salt and cracked black pepper. Mix together well.

Drizzle a little of the dressing over each oyster and serve with the cubes of brown bread.

Olive tapenade

PREPARATION *10 minutes*
MAKES *1½ cups*

400 g (14 oz/2⅓ cups) pitted
  kalamata olives

2 garlic cloves, crushed

2 anchovy fillets in oil,
  drained

2 tablespoons capers in
  brine, rinsed, squeezed dry

2 teaspoons chopped fresh
  thyme

2 teaspoons dijon mustard

1 tablespoon lemon juice

60 ml (2 fl oz/¼ cup) olive
  oil

1 tablespoon brandy, optional

Place the kalamata olives, the crushed garlic, anchovies, capers,
chopped thyme, dijon mustard, lemon juice, olive oil and
brandy in a food processor and process until smooth. Season
to taste with salt and freshly ground black pepper. Spoon
into a clean, warm jar, cover with a layer of olive oil, seal and
refrigerate for up to 1 week. Serve on bruschetta or with a meze
plate.

Note: When refrigerated, the olive oil may solidify, making
it an opaque white colour. This is a property of olive oil and
will not affect the flavour of the dish. Simply bring the dish to
room temperature before serving and the olive oil with return
to a liquid state.

Salt and pepper squid

PREPARATION *15 minutes + chilling time*
COOKING *10 minutes* SERVES *12*

1 kg squid tubes, halved lengthways (see Note)

250 ml (9 fl oz/ 1 cup) lemon juice

125 g (4½ fl oz/ 1 cup) cornflour (cornstarch)

1½ tablespoons salt

1 tablespoon ground white pepper

2 teaspoons caster (superfine) sugar

4 egg whites, lightly beaten

oil, for deep-frying

lemon wedges, for serving

Open out the squid tubes, then wash and pat them dry. Lay on a chopping board with the inside facing upwards. Score a fine diamond pattern on the inside, being careful not to cut all the way through. Cut the squid into pieces measuring 5 cm x 2 cm (2 inch x 2 inch). Place in a flat non-metallic dish and pour on the lemon juice. Cover and then refrigerate for 15 minutes. Drain well and pat dry.

Combine the cornflour, salt, white pepper and sugar in a bowl. Dip the squid into the egg white and lightly coat with the cornflour mixture, shaking off any excess.

Fill a deep heavy-based saucepan or deep-fryer one-third full of oil and heat to 180°C (350°F), or until a cube of bread dropped into the oil turns golden brown in 15 seconds. Deep-fry the squid, in batches, for 1 minute each batch, or until the squid turns lightly golden and curls up. Drain on crumpled paper towels. Serve with lemon wedges.

Note: If you are cleaning the squid yourself, reserve the tentacles, cut them into groups of two or three depending on the size; marinate and cook them with the tubes.

Grissini wrapped in smoked salmon

PREPARATION *20 minutes*

MAKES *24*

125 g (4½ oz) cream cheese, at room temperature

1–2 tablespoons dill, chopped

¼ teaspoon lemon zest, finely grated

24 ready-made grissini

8–10 slices smoked salmon, cut into thin strips

Mix the cream cheese, the fresh dill and lemon zest in a bowl until the dill is well distributed. Season, to taste, with salt. Spread some of the cream cheese mixture onto three-quarters of each length of grissini. Wrap the salmon around the stick, over the cheese, securing it with more cheese. Repeat with the remaining grissini.

Prepare grissini close to serving (up to about 30 minutes before) as the biscuits will start to soften once the cheese is spread on them.

Salt cod fritters

PREPARATION *15 minutes + soaking time*
COOKING *45 minutes* MAKES *about 36*

500 g (1 lb 2 oz) bacalao (salt
cod)

1 large all-purpose potato,
such as desiree, (200 g/
7 oz), unpeeled

2 tablespoons milk

60 ml (2 fl oz/¼ cup) olive
oil

1 small white onion, finely
chopped

2 garlic cloves, crushed

30 g (1 oz/¼ cup) self-raising
flour

2 eggs, separated

1 tablespoon flat-leaf
(Italian) parsley, chopped

Soak the bacalao in plenty of cold water in the fridge for about 20 hours, changing the water four or five times to remove the excess saltiness.

Cook potato in a saucepan of boiling water for 20 minutes, or until soft. When cool, peel and mash the potato with the milk and 2 tablespoons of the olive oil.

Drain the bacalao, cut into large pieces and put in a saucepan. Cover with water, bring to the boil over high heat, then reduce the heat to medium and cook for 10 minutes, or until the fish is soft and there is a froth on the surface. Drain. When cool enough to handle, remove the skin and any bones, then mash the flesh well with a fork until flaky.

Heat the remaining oil in a small frying pan and cook the onion over medium heat for 5 minutes, or until softened and starting to brown. Add the garlic and cook for 1 minute. Remove from the heat.

Combine the potato, the bacalao, the onion and garlic, flour, egg yolks and the parsley in a bowl and season. Whisk the egg whites until stiff, then fold into the mixture. Fill a deep-fryer or large heavy-based saucepan one-third full of olive oil and heat to 190°C (375°F), or until a cube of bread dropped into the oil browns in 10 seconds. Drop heaped tablespoons of the mixture into oil and cook, turning once, for 2–3 minutes, or until puffed and golden. Drain well and serve immediately.

Fried calamari

PREPARATION *10 minutes*
COOKING *10 minutes*   SERVES *4-6*

500 g (1 lb 2 oz) squid tubes, cleaned

185 g (6½ oz/1½ cups) plain (all-purpose) flour

2 teaspoons sweet paprika (pimentón)

olive oil, for deep-frying

lemon wedges, to serve

allioli (see page 111) or ready-made garlic mayonnaise or sauce, to serve

Wash the calamari and cut into rings about 1 cm (½ inch) wide. Combine flour and paprika. Season the calamari rings well with salt and pepper and toss in the flour to lightly coat.

Fill a deep, heavy-based saucepan one-third full of oil and heat to 180°C (350°F), or until a cube of bread dropped into the oil browns in 15 seconds. Add the calamari in batches and cook for 2 minutes, or until golden. Drain and serve hot with the lemon wedges and allioli if desired.

Prawns with romesco sauce

PREPARATION 30 minutes + chilling time
COOKING 35 minutes SERVES 6-8

30 large, raw prawns (shrimp)

1 tablespoon olive oil

Romesco sauce

4 garlic cloves, unpeeled

1 roma (plum) tomato, halved and seeded

2 long red chillies

2 tablespoons whole blanched almonds

2 tablespoons hazelnuts

60 g (2¼ oz) sun-dried capsicums (peppers) in oil

1 tablespoon olive oil

1 tablespoon red wine vinegar

Peel prawns, leaving the tails intact. Cut down the back and gently pull out the dark vein, starting at the head end. Mix prawns with ¼ teaspoon salt and refrigerate for 30 minutes.

To make romesco sauce, preheat the oven to 200°C (400°F/ Gas 6). Wrap garlic cloves in foil, put on a baking tray with tomato and chillies and bake for about 12 minutes. Spread the almonds and hazelnuts on the tray and bake for another 3–5 minutes. Leave to cool for 15 minutes. Peel the skin off the tomato.

Transfer almonds and hazelnuts to a small blender or food processor and blend until finely ground. Squeeze the garlic, and the tomato flesh, into the blender, discarding the skins. Split the chillies and remove the seeds. Scrape the flesh into the blender, discarding the skins. Pat the capsicums dry with paper towel, then chop them and add to the blender along with oil, vinegar, some salt and 2 tablespoons water. Blend until smooth, adding more water, if necessary, to form a soft dipping consistency. Set aside for 30 minutes.

Heat the olive oil in a frying pan over high heat and cook the prawns for 5 minutes, or until curled up and slightly pink. Serve with the sauce.

The little TAPAS book

Vegetarian

Tortilla

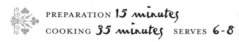

PREPARATION *15 minutes*
COOKING *35 minutes* SERVES *6-8*

500 g (1 lb 2 oz) all-purpose
  potatoes, peeled and cut
  into 1 cm (½ inch) slices

60 ml (2 fl oz/¼ cup) olive
  oil

1 brown onion, thinly sliced

4 garlic cloves, thinly sliced

2 tablespoons finely chopped
  flat-leaf (Italian) parsley

6 eggs

Put the potato slices in a large saucepan, cover with cold water
and bring to the boil over high heat. Boil for 5 minutes, then
drain and set aside.

Heat oil in a deep-sided non-stick frying pan over medium
heat. Add onion and garlic and cook for 5 minutes, or until
the onion softens.

Add the potato and parsley to the pan and stir to combine.
Cook over medium heat for 5 minutes, gently pressing down
into the pan.

Whisk the eggs with 1 teaspoon each of salt and freshly ground
black pepper and pour evenly over the potato. Cover and cook
over low–medium heat for 20 minutes, or until the eggs are
just set. Slide onto a serving plate or serve directly from pan.

Fried potatoes with garlic mayonnaise (allioli)

PREPARATION 20 minutes   COOKING 45 minutes
SERVES 4-6   ALLIOLI MAKES 250ml (9 fl oz/1 cup)

750 g (1 lb 10 oz) all-purpose
  potatoes, peeled
60 ml (2 fl oz/¼ cup) olive
  oil

Allioli
2 egg yolks
4 garlic cloves, crushed
60 ml (2 fl oz/¼ cup) white
  wine vinegar or lemon juice
250 ml (8 fl oz/1 cup) mild
  olive oil

To make allioli, put egg yolks, garlic and half of the vinegar
or lemon juice in a bowl. Using a balloon whisk, or electric
beaters, whisk until well combined. While you continuously
whisk, gradually add the oil in a slow stream until a thick
mayonnaise forms. If it becomes too thick, add remaining
vinegar and continue adding the rest of the oil. Season well.

Preheat oven to 200°C (400°F/Gas 6). Cut the potatoes into
4 cm (1½ inch) cubes and put on a baking tray with olive oil.
Mix to coat and season well. Cook in the oven for 45 minutes,
or until golden. Season potatoes and serve with allioli.

Note: Allioli can be kept in the refrigerator in an airtight
container for up to 2–3 days.

Chargrilled vegetable skewers

PREPARATION *20 minutes + soaking time*
COOKING *30 minutes* MAKES *24*

Charbroiled vegetable skewers

12 white mushrooms,
   cut in half

1 yellow capsicum (pepper)

1 red capsicum (pepper)

1 zucchini

1 small red onion

24 bay leaves

250 ml (9 fl oz/1 cup) olive oil

2 tablespoons lemon juice

1 garlic clove, crushed

2 teaspoons thyme leaves

Concassé

1 tablespoon olive oil

1 small onion, finely chopped

1 garlic clove, crushed

425 g (15 oz) can chopped
   tomatoes

4 tablespoons torn basil

Soak twenty-four wooden skewers in water for 1 hour.

Cut the yellow and red capsicums, zuchinni and onion into 2 cm (¾ inch) pieces. Thread each skewer with a piece of mushroom, pieces of yellow and red capsicum, zucchini, onion, and a bay leaf, then put in a large, flat nonmetallic dish and season well with salt and cracked black pepper.

Put the olive oil, lemon juice, garlic, and thyme in a small bowl and mix together. Pour over the skewers and marinate for 20 minutes.

Meanwhile, to make concassé, heat the oil in a small saucepan over medium heat, add the onion, and cook for 5 minutes or until soft. Stir in the garlic and cook for 30 seconds, then add the tomatoes. Simmer for 10–15 minutes, then add the basil.

Cook the skewers on a hot barbecue grill or charbroil pan for 3 minutes on each side or until golden, brushing occasionally with the marinade. Serve with the concassé.

Broad bean dip

PREPARATION 20 minutes + soaking time
COOKING 1 hour 15 minutes SERVES 6

175 g (6 oz/1¼ cups) dried broad (fava) beans or ready-skinned dried broad beans

2 garlic cloves, crushed

½ teaspoon ground cumin

1½ tablespoons lemon juice

80 ml (2½ fl oz/⅓ cup) olive oil

large pinch of paprika

2 tablespoons chopped flat-leaf (Italian) parsley

flatbread, to serve

Put the dried broad beans in a large bowl, cover with 750 ml (26 fl oz/3 cups) cold water and leave to soak in a cool place. If using dried beans with skins, soak them for 48 hours, changing the water once. If using ready-skinned dried beans, soak them for 12 hours only.

Drain beans. If using beans with skins, remove skins by slitting the skin with the point of a knife and slipping the bean out.

Put beans in a large saucepan with water to cover and bring to the boil. Cover and simmer over low heat for 1 hour, or until tender (if the water boils over, uncover the pan a little). After 1 hour, remove lid and cook for a further 15 minutes, or until most of the liquid has evaporated, taking care that the beans do not catch on the base of the pan.

Purée the beans in a food processsor, then transfer to a bowl and stir in garlic, cumin and lemon juice. Add salt, to taste. Gradually stir in enough olive oil to give a spreadable or thick dipping consistency, starting with half the oil. As the mixture cools it may become thicker, in which case you can stir through a little warm water to return mixture to a softer consistency.

Spread the purée over a large dish and sprinkle with paprika and parsley. Serve with flat bread.

Fried chickpeas

PREPARATION *30 minutes*
COOKING *15 minutes* SERVES *6-8*

300 g (10½ oz) dried
  chickpeas
oil, for deep-frying
½ teaspoon mild or hot
  paprika
¼ teaspoon cayenne pepper

Put chickpeas in a large bowl, cover with plenty of cold water
and soak overnight. Drain well and pat dry with paper towel.

Fill a deep heavy-based saucepan one-third full of oil and heat
to 180°C (350°F), or until a cube of bread dropped into the
oil browns in 15 seconds. Deep-fry half of the chickpeas for
3 minutes. Remove with a slotted spoon. Drain on crumpled
paper towel and repeat with the rest of the chickpeas. Partially
cover pan as some chickpeas may pop. Do not leave oil on the
heat unattended.

Reheat oil and fry the chickpeas again in batches for 3 minutes
each batch, or until browned. Drain. Season the paprika with
the cayenne pepper and some salt, and sprinkle over the hot
chickpeas. Leave to cool and serve.

Spanish pizza

PREPARATION *30 minutes*　COOKING *45 minutes*　SERVES *4-6*

Base

2 teaspoons dried yeast

1 teaspoon caster (superfine) sugar

280 g (10 oz/2¼ cups) plain (all-purpose) flour

Topping

10 English spinach leaves, shredded

1 tablespoon olive oil

2 garlic cloves, crushed

2 onions, chopped

440 g (15½ oz) drained and crushed tinned tomatoes

12 black olives, pitted and chopped

Preheat oven to 210°C (415°F/Gas 6–7). Brush a 25 x 30 cm (10 x 12 inch) Swiss roll tin (jelly roll tin) with melted butter or oil.

To make the base, combine the yeast, sugar and flour in a large bowl. Gradually add 250 ml (9 fl oz/1 cup) warm water and blend until smooth. Knead the dough on a lightly floured surface until it is smooth and elastic. Place in a lightly oiled bowl, cover with a tea towel (dish towel) and leave to rise in a warm position for 15 minutes, or until the dough has almost doubled in size.

To make topping, put the spinach in a large saucepan, cover and cook on low heat for 3 minutes. Drain the spinach and cool. Squeeze out the excess moisture with your hands and set the spinach aside.

Heat the oil in a frying pan and add the garlic and onions. Cook over low heat for 5–6 minutes. Add the tomatoes and ¼ teaspoon ground pepper and simmer gently for 5 minutes.

Punch the dough down, remove from the bowl and knead on a lightly floured board for 2–3 minutes. Roll the dough out and fit it in the tin. Spread with spinach, top with the tomato mixture and sprinkle the olives on top.

Bake for 25–30 minutes. Cut into small squares or fingers. The pizza can be served hot or cold.

Marinated capsicums

PREPARATION *15 minutes + marinating time* SERVES **6**

3 red capsicums (peppers), roasted

3 thyme sprigs

I garlic clove, thinly sliced

2 teaspoons roughly chopped flat-leaf (Italian) parsley

I bay leaf

I spring onion (scallion), sliced

I teaspoon sweet paprika (pimentón)

60 ml (2 fl oz/¼ cup) extra virgin olive oil

Marinated capsicums (peppers)

Slice capsicums thinly, then place in a bowl with the thyme, garlic, parsley, bay leaf and spring onion. Mix well.

Whisk together paprika, oil, vinegar and season with salt and pepper. Pour over the capsicum mixture and toss to combine. Cover and then refrigerate for at least 3 hours, stirring once or twice during this period, or preferably overnight. Remove from the refrigerator about 30 minutes before serving.

Roasted capsicums (peppers)

Cut each capsicum (pepper) into four flattish pieces and carefully remove the seeds and membrane. Arrange the pieces in a single layer on a baking tray and cook under a hot grill (broiler) until the skins are blackened and blistered.

Put the peppers in a large bowl and cover with plastic wrap (or put them in a plastic bag) and leave to cool for 10 minutes.

Peel away the skins and cut the flesh into thin strips.

Polenta chillies

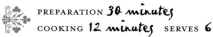

PREPARATION **30 minutes**
COOKING **12 minutes** SERVES **6**

330 g (11¾ oz) jar mild,
whole chillies

60 g (2¼ oz/½ cup) grated
cheddar

100 g (3½ oz) soft cream
cheese

40 g (1½ oz/⅓ cup) plain
(all-purpose) flour

2 eggs, lightly beaten

110 g (3¾ oz/¾ cup) polenta

75 g (2¾ oz/¾ cup) dry
breadcrumbs

oil, for deep-frying

sour cream, to serve

Select 12 large, similar-sized chillies from the jar. Drain well
and dry with paper towel. With a sharp knife, cut a slit down
length of one side of each chilli. Remove all seeds and the
membrane. Combine grated cheddar and cream cheese, then
fill each chilli with the cheese mixture.

Put the flour onto a large plate and the beaten eggs in a small
bowl. Combine the polenta and breadcrumbs in a small plastic
bag, then transfer to a large plate. Roll each chilli in the flour,
shake off the excess, dip in egg, then roll in the breadcrumb
mixture to coat chillies. Refrigerate for 1 hour. Re-dip in egg
and re-roll in breadcrumbs. Return to refrigerator for 1 hour.

Fill a heavy-based saucepan one-third full of oil and heat oil to
180°c (350°F), or until a cube of bread dropped into the oil
browns in 15 seconds. Deep-fry chillies in small batches until
golden and drain on paper towel. Serve with sour cream.

Sweet and salty nuts

PREPARATION *20 minutes*
COOKING *15 minutes* SERVES *6-8*

250 g (9 oz/1²/₃ cups)
  blanched almonds
250 g (9 oz/2½ cups) pecans
55 g (2 oz/¼ cup) sugar

I teaspoon ground cinnamon
pinch ground cloves
½ teaspoon curry powder
¼ teaspoon ground cumin

Preheat the oven to 180°C (350°F/Gas 4). Spread the almonds and pecans on a large baking tray and bake for 5–10 minutes, or until they are crisp and lightly coloured. Remove and allow to cool.

Combine the sugar, spices, I teaspoon salt and ½ teaspoon ground pepper in a small bowl and mix well.

Heat a large non-stick frying pan over medium heat and add almonds and pecans. Sprinkle spice mixture over nuts and stir for 5 minutes, or until nuts turn golden. The sugar will melt and coat nuts. Gently shake frying pan often to ensure even cooking. If nuts stick together, separate with a wooden spoon. When nuts are cooked, remove from heat and spread them on a lightly oiled baking tray to cool.

Notes: If you use a small frying pan, cook the nuts in batches. Cashew nuts, macadamia nuts or peanuts can be used or, if you prefer, just one variety. Transfer the cooled nuts to tightly sealed jars or containers. They will keep for a few weeks.

Fried potato cakes

PREPARATION *20 minutes + cooling time*
COOKING *40 minutes* MAKES *8*

600 g (1 lb 5 oz) potatoes

2 garlic cloves, unpeeled

1½ teaspoons ground cumin

½ teaspoon ground coriander

1 teaspoon paprika

⅛ teaspoon cayenne pepper

2 tablespoons flat-leaf (Italian) parsley, finely chopped

2 tablespoons finely chopped coriander (cilantro) leaves

2 small eggs

oil for frying

Peel potatoes, cut in thick slices and place in a saucepan with water to cover. Add the garlic and bring to the boil. Boil for 15—20 minutes until tender, drain and return to medium heat to dry potatoes. Squeeze pulp from garlic cloves into potatoes, then mash. Add spices. Mix in and leave until cool.

Add parsley, coriander leaves and one egg to the mash and season to taste. Mix well without overworking. Divide into 8 even portions and shape into smooth cakes 1.5 cm (½ inch) thick and 8 cm (3¼ inches) in diameter. Place on a baking paper-lined baking tray. Beat remaining egg in a shallow dish. In a frying pan, add oil to a depth of 5 mm (¼ inch), and place over medium—high heat. When hot, dip cakes into the egg to coat and fry for 2—3 minutes each side or until golden and heated through. Drain on paper towel and serve hot.

Chilli olives

PREPARATION 15 minutes + soaking and marinating time
FILLS 1 litre (35 fl oz/4 cup) jar

3 garlic cloves, thinly sliced

2 tablespoons vinegar or
  lemon juice

500 g (1 lb 2 oz) black olives,
  cured (wrinkled)

1 handful chopped
  flat-leaf (Italian) parsley

1 tablespoon chilli flakes

3 teaspoons coriander seeds,
  crushed

2 teaspoons cumin seeds,
  crushed

500 ml (17 fl oz/2 cups) olive
  oil

Soak garlic slices in the vinegar or lemon juice for 24 hours.
Drain and mix in a bowl with the olives, parsley, chilli flakes,
coriander and cumin.

Sterilise a 1 litre (35 fl oz/4 cups) wide-necked jar by rinsing it
with boiling water, then drying it in a warm oven. Don't dry it
with a tea towel (dish towel).

Spoon olives into the jar and pour in the olive oil. Seal and
marinate in the refrigerator for 1–2 weeks before serving at
room temperature. The olives will keep for a further month
in the refrigerator.

Warm artichoke dip

PREPARATION *10 minutes* COOKING *15 minutes*
MAKES *500 g* (11 lb 2 oz/4 cups)

2 x 400 g (14 oz) cans
artichoke hearts, drained

250 g (9 oz/I cup) whole-egg
mayonnaise

75 g (2½ oz/¾ cup) grated
parmesan

2 teaspoons onion flakes

2 tablespoons grated
parmesan, extra

ground paprika, to garnish

Preheat the oven to moderate 180°C (350°F/Gas 4). Squeeze
the artichokes to remove any liquid. Chop finely and combine
with the mayonnaise, parmesan and onion flakes. Spread into
a shallow I litre ovenproof dish.

Sprinkle with extra parmesan and paprika and then bake for
15 minutes, or until lightly browned and heated through.
Serve hot with dippers such as puff-pastry twists or crusty
French bread.

Spinach and feta triangles

PREPARATION *25 minutes* COOKING *40 minutes* MAKES *8*

1 kg (2 lb 4 oz) English spinach

60 ml (2 fl oz/¼ cup) olive oil

1 onion, chopped

10 spring onions, sliced

20 g (¾ oz/⅓ cup) chopped fresh parsley

1 tablespoon chopped fresh dill

large pinch of ground nutmeg

35 g (1¼ oz/⅓ cup) grated parmesan

150 g crumbled feta cheese

90 g ricotta cheese

4 eggs, lightly beaten

40 g butter, melted

1 tablespoon olive oil, extra

12 sheets filo pastry

Trim any stems from the spinach. Wash leaves, roughly chop and place in a large pan with a little water clinging to leaves. Cover and then cook over low heat for 5 minutes, or until the leaves have wilted. Drain well and allow to cool slightly before squeezing to remove the excess water.

Heat oil in a heavy-based frying pan. Add onion and cook over low heat for 10 minutes, or until tender and golden. Add the spring onion and cook for a further 3 minutes. Remove from the heat. Stir in spinach, parsley, dill, nutmeg, parmesan, feta, ricotta and egg. Season well.

Preheat the oven to moderate 180°C (350°F/Gas 4). Grease two baking trays. Combine the butter with the extra oil. Work with three sheets of pastry at a time, covering the rest with a damp tea towel. Brush each sheet with butter mixture and lay them on top of each other. Halve lengthways.

Place 4 tablespoons of filling on an angle at the end of each strip. Fold the pastry to enclose the filling and form a triangle. Continue folding the triangle over until you reach the end. Brush with the remaining butter mixture and then bake for 20 minutes, or until golden brown.

Mushrooms with two sauces

PREPARATION 30 minutes COOKING 10 minutes SERVES 8

750 g (1 lb 10 oz) button
  mushrooms

40 g (1½ oz/⅓ cup) plain
  (all-purpose) flour

100 g (3½ oz/1 cup) dry
  breadcrumbs

3 eggs

olive oil, for deep-frying

Sauces

1 small red capsicum (pepper)

2 egg yolks

1 teaspoon dijon mustard

1 tablespoon lemon juice

250 ml (9 fl oz/1 cup) olive oil

1 small garlic clove, crushed

2 tablespoons plain yoghurt

2 teaspoons finely chopped
  flat-leaf (Italian) parsley

Wipe the mushrooms with paper towels and remove the stems. Measure the flour into a large plastic bag and the breadcrumbs into a separate bag. Lightly beat the eggs in a bowl.

Put mushrooms in with flour and shake until evenly coated. Shake off any excess flour, then dip half the mushrooms in egg to coat well. Transfer to the bag with breadcrumbs and shake to cover thoroughly. Place on a tray covered with baking paper. Repeat with remaining mushrooms. Refrigerate for 1 hour.

Cut capsicum into large flattish pieces, discarding membranes and the seeds. Cook, skin-side-up, under a hot grill (broiler) until the skin blackens and blisters. Cool in a plastic bag, then peel. Process in a food processor or blender to a smooth paste.

Place the egg yolks, mustard and half the lemon juice in a bowl. Beat together for 1 minute using electric beaters. Add oil, a teaspoon at a time, beating constantly until the mixture is thick and creamy. Continue beating until all oil is added, then add remaining lemon juice. Divide mayonnaise between two bowls. Into one, stir garlic, yoghurt and parsley and into the other, the red capsicum mixture.

Fill a heavy-based saucepan one-third full of oil and heat oil to 180°C (350°F), or until a cube of bread dropped into the oil browns in 15 seconds. Gently lower batches of mushrooms into the oil and cook for 1–2 minutes, or until golden brown. Remove with a slotted spoon and drain on paper towels.

To serve, arrange mushrooms on serving plates and fill each mushroom with either of the sauces. If you prefer, you can spoon a little of each sauce into each mushroom.

Note: Cook the mushrooms just before serving. The sauces can be made up to 1 day ahead and refrigerated, covered.

IN·MANU·EJUS·POTESTAS·ET·IMPERIUM

Cheese fritters

175 g (6 oz) block firm feta
  cheese

125 g (4½ oz) mozzarella
  cheese

40 g (1½ oz/⅓ cup) plain
  (all-purpose) flour

1 egg, beaten

50 g (1¾ oz/½ cup) dry
  breadcrumbs

oil, for pan-frying

Cut feta and mozzarella into 2 cm (¾ inch) cubes. Combine
the flour and ¼ teaspoon black pepper on a sheet of baking
paper. Toss the cheese lightly in the seasoned flour and shake
off the excess.

Dip the cheese into the egg a few pieces at a time. Coat with the
breadcrumbs and shake off the excess. Repeat process with the
remaining cheese and crumbs. Arrange on a foil-lined baking
tray and refrigerate, covered, for 25 minutes.

Heat 3 cm (1¼ inches) oil in a deep frying pan to 180°C
(350°F), or until a cube of bread dropped into the oil turns
golden brown in 15 seconds. Cook a few pieces of cheese at a
time over medium heat, for 2–3 minutes each batch, or until
golden and crisp. Drain on crumpled paper towels. Serve with
sweet chilli, plum or cranberry sauce.

Potatoes in spicy tomato sauce

PREPARATION *25 minutes* COOKING *45 minutes* SERVES **6**

1 kg (2 lb 4 oz) all-purpose potatoes, such as desiree

oil, for deep-frying

2 tablespoons olive oil

¼ red onion, finely chopped

2 garlic cloves, crushed

3 teaspoons sweet paprika (pimentón)

¼ teaspoon cayenne pepper

500 g (1 lb 2 oz) ripe roma (plum) tomatoes

1 bay leaf

1 teaspoon white sugar

Score a cross in the base of each tomato with a knife. Put the tomatoes in a bowl of boiling water for 10 seconds, then plunge them into a bowl of cold water. Remove from water and peel skin away from cross—it should slip off easily. If desired, remove the seeds with a teaspoon, and chop flesh.

Peel, then cut the potatoes into 2 cm (¾ inch) cubes. Rinse, then drain well and pat completely dry. Fill a deep-fryer or large heavy-based saucepan one-third full of oil and heat to 180°C (350°F), or until a cube of bread dropped into the oil browns in 15 seconds. Cook potato in batches for 5 minutes, or until golden. Drain well on paper towel. Do not discard oil.

Heat olive oil in a saucepan over medium heat and cook onion for 5 minutes, or until softened. Add the garlic, paprika and cayenne pepper and cook for 1–2 minutes, or until fragrant.

Add the tomato, bay leaf, sugar and 80 ml (2½ fl oz/1/16 cup) water and cook, stirring occasionally, for 20 minutes, or until thick and pulpy. Cool slightly and remove bay leaf. Blend in a food processor until smooth, adding a little water if necessary. Before serving, return sauce to the saucepan and simmer over low heat for 2 minutes, or until heated through. Season well.

Reheat oil to 180°C (350°F) and cook potato again, in batches, for 2 minutes, or until very crisp and golden. Drain on paper towel. This second frying makes potato extra crispy and stops sauce soaking in immediately. Put on a platter and cover with sauce. Serve immediately.

Olive basil cheese spread

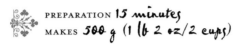

PREPARATION **15 minutes**
MAKES **500 g** (1 lb 2 oz/2 cups)

250 g (9 oz/1 cup) cream
  cheese, softened

200 g (7 oz) feta cheese

20 g (¾ oz) basil leaves

60 ml (2 fl oz/¼ cup) olive
  oil

15 kalamata olives, pitted and
  roughly chopped

crusty bread, to serve

Combine the cream cheese, feta, basil, 1 tablespoon of the oil
and ¼ teaspoon cracked black pepper in a bowl and then mix
until smooth.

Fold in the olives and spoon into a serving bowl. Smooth the
top with the back of the spoon and pour the remaining oil over
the top. Garnish with a little more cracked pepper and serve
with crusty bread.

Zucchini and haloumi fritters

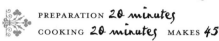
PREPARATION 20 minutes
COOKING 20 minutes MAKES 45

300 g (10½ oz) zucchini
   (courgette)

4 spring onions, thinly sliced

200 g (7 oz) haloumi cheese,
   coarsely grated

30 g (1 oz/¼ cup) plain
   (all-purpose) flour

2 eggs

I tablespoon chopped fresh
   dill, plus sprigs, to garnish

60 ml (2 fl oz/¼ cup) oil

I lemon, cut into very thin
   slices, seeds removed

90 g (3¼ oz/⅓ cup) thick
   Greek-style yoghurt

Coarsely grate the zucchini and squeeze out as much liquid
as possible in your hands. Combine the zucchini with spring
onion, haloumi, flour, eggs and dill. Season well.

Heat the oil in a large heavy-based frying pan. Form fritters
(using heaped teaspoons of the mixture) and cook in batches
for 2 minutes each side, or until golden and firm. Drain on
crumpled paper towels.

Cut each slice of lemon into quarters to make small triangles.
Top each fritter with ½ teaspoon yoghurt, a piece of lemon
and a small sprig of dill.

Stuffed chillies

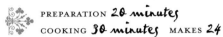

PREPARATION *20 minutes*
COOKING *30 minutes* MAKES *24*

I teaspoon cumin seeds

12 small mild jalapeño or similar mild rectangular-shaped fat chillies, approx. 4 cm x 3 cm (1½ inch x 1¼ inch)

I tablespoon olive oil

2 garlic cloves, finely chopped

½ small red onion, finely chopped

125 g (4½ oz/½ cup) cream cheese, softened

30 g (1 oz/¼ cup) coarsely grated cheddar

2 tablespoons finely chopped drained sun-dried tomatoes

I tablespoon chopped fresh coriander (cilantro) leaves

I teaspoon finely chopped lime zest

pinch of smoked paprika

50 g (¾ oz /1½ cups) coarse dry breadcrumbs

2 teaspoons lime juice

coriander (cilantro) leaves, to garnish

Preheat the oven to 200°C (400°F/Gas 6). Line a baking tray with baking paper. Toast the cumin seeds in a dry frying pan for 1–2 minutes, or until fragrant. Cool slightly, then grind the seeds.

Cut chillies lengthways through the middle. Wearing gloves, remove seeds and membranes. Bring a saucepan of water to the boil, add the chillies and cook for 1 minute, or until water comes back to the boil. Drain, rinse under cold water, then return to a saucepan of fresh boiling water for another minute before draining, rinsing, then draining again.

Heat the oil in a non-stick frying pan and cook the garlic and onion over medium–low heat for 4–5 minutes, or until onion softens. Mash cream cheese in a bowl, add cheddar, sun-dried tomato, the coriander, lime zest, the paprika, cumin and half the breadcrumbs, and mix well. Stir in onion and season. Fill each chilli with one heaped teaspoon of the mixture, then lay on the baking tray and scatter with remaining breadcrumbs.

Bake for 20 minutes. Squeeze some lime juice over the top and garnish with coriander leaves.

Mini focaccia with roasted vegetables

 PREPARATION *20 minutes*
COOKING *35 minutes* MAKES *24*

2 red capsicums (peppers)

2 yellow capsicums (peppers)

3 slender eggplants
(aubergines)

2 large zucchini (courgettes)

1 red onion

80 ml (2½ fl oz/⅓ cup) extra
virgin olive oil

3 garlic cloves, crushed

12 mini focaccias, halved

60 g (2¼ oz/¼ cup) ready-
made pesto

3 large bocconcini, sliced

Preheat the oven to 200°C (400°F/Gas 6). Cut the red and
yellow capsicums into 3 cm (1¼ inch) pieces. Slice eggplants
and zucchini into 1 cm (½ inch) rounds, then thinly slice the
onion. Place all the vegetables in a roasting tin with the oil and
garlic, then season well and toss together thoroughly. Roast for
25 minutes, or until cooked.

Spread each half of the focaccia with ½ teaspoon of pesto and
divide vegetables among them. Place two slices of bocconcini
on top of each base, then top with the lid. Toast focaccias on
both sides on a hot chargrill pan until heated through. Slice
each focaccia in half, then wrap a 3 cm (1¼ inch) wide band
of double greaseproof paper around middle of sandwiches and
secure with string. Serve warm.

Tomato and haloumi skewers

 PREPARATION *30 minutes*
COOKING ~~10~~ MAKES *22*

500 g (1 lb 2 oz) haloumi
cheese

5 large handfuls basil

150 g (5½ oz) semi-dried
(sun-blushed) tomatoes

2 tablespoons balsamic
vinegar

2 tablespoons extra virgin
olive oil

1 teaspoon sea salt

Preheat a barbecue hotplate or chargrill pan. Cut the cheese
into 1.5 cm (5/8 inch) pieces. Thread a basil leaf onto a small
skewer, followed by a piece of haloumi, a semi-dried tomato,
another piece of haloumi and another basil leaf. Repeat to use
the remaining ingredients.

Place the skewers on the barbecue hotplate and cook, turning
occasionally until the cheese is golden brown, brushing with
the combined vinegar and oil while cooking. Sprinkle with salt
and serve hot or warm.

Toast with tomato

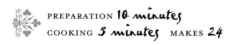

PREPARATION **10 minutes**
COOKING **5 minutes**   MAKES **24**

1 crusty bread stick

6 garlic cloves, halved

3 tomatoes, halved

**extra virgin olive oil, for
  drizzling**

Slice the bread stick diagonally and toast the slices very lightly.
Rub them on one side with a cut garlic clove, then with half a
tomato, squeezing the juice onto the bread. Season with a little
salt and drizzle with extra virgin olive oil.

Bondas

2 teaspoons vegetable oil

1 teaspoon brown mustard seeds

1 onion, finely chopped

2 teaspoons grated fresh ginger

4 curry leaves

3 small green chillies, finely chopped

1.25 kg (2 lb 12 oz) potatoes (all-purpose), diced and cooked

pinch ground turmeric

2 tablespoons lemon juice

20 g (¾ oz/⅓ cup) chopped coriander (cilantro) leaves

oil, for deep-frying

Batter

110 g (3¾ oz/1 cup) besan (chickpea flour)

30 g (1 oz/¼ cup) self-raising flour

45 g (1¾ oz/¼ cup) rice flour

¼ teaspoon ground turmeric

1 teaspoon chilli powder

Heat a wok over medium heat. Add the oil and swirl to coat the base and side. Add mustard seeds and stir for 30 seconds, or until fragrant. Add onion, ginger, curry leaves and chilli and cook for 2 minutes. Add the potato, turmeric and 2 teaspoons water and stir for 2 minutes, or until mixture is dry. Remove from the heat and cool. Stir in the lemon juice and coriander leaves, then season to taste. Shape into 24 balls, using 1 heaped tablespoon of the mixture for each ball.

To make the batter, sift the flours, turmeric, chilli powder and ¼ teaspoon salt into a bowl. Make a well in the centre. Gradually whisk in 330 ml (11¼ fl oz/1⅓ cups) water to make a smooth batter.

Fill a wok one-third full of oil and heat to 180°C (350°F), or until a cube of bread dropped into oil browns in 15 seconds. Dip balls into the batter, then cook in the hot oil, in batches, for 1–2 minutes, or until golden. Drain on crumpled paper towel and season with salt. Serve hot.

Stuffed black olives

PREPARATION 15 minutes + chilling time
COOKING 15 minutes MAKES 36

36 pitted jumbo black or
large kalamata olives (see
Note)

100 g (3½ oz) goat's cheese

1 teaspoon capers, drained
and finely chopped

1 clove garlic, crushed

1 tablespoon chopped fresh
flat-leaf parsley

1½ tablespoons plain (all-
purpose) flour

2 eggs, lightly beaten

100 g (3½ oz/1 cup) dry
breadcrumbs

1 tablespoon finely chopped
fresh flat-leaf (Italian)
parsley, extra

oil, for deep-frying

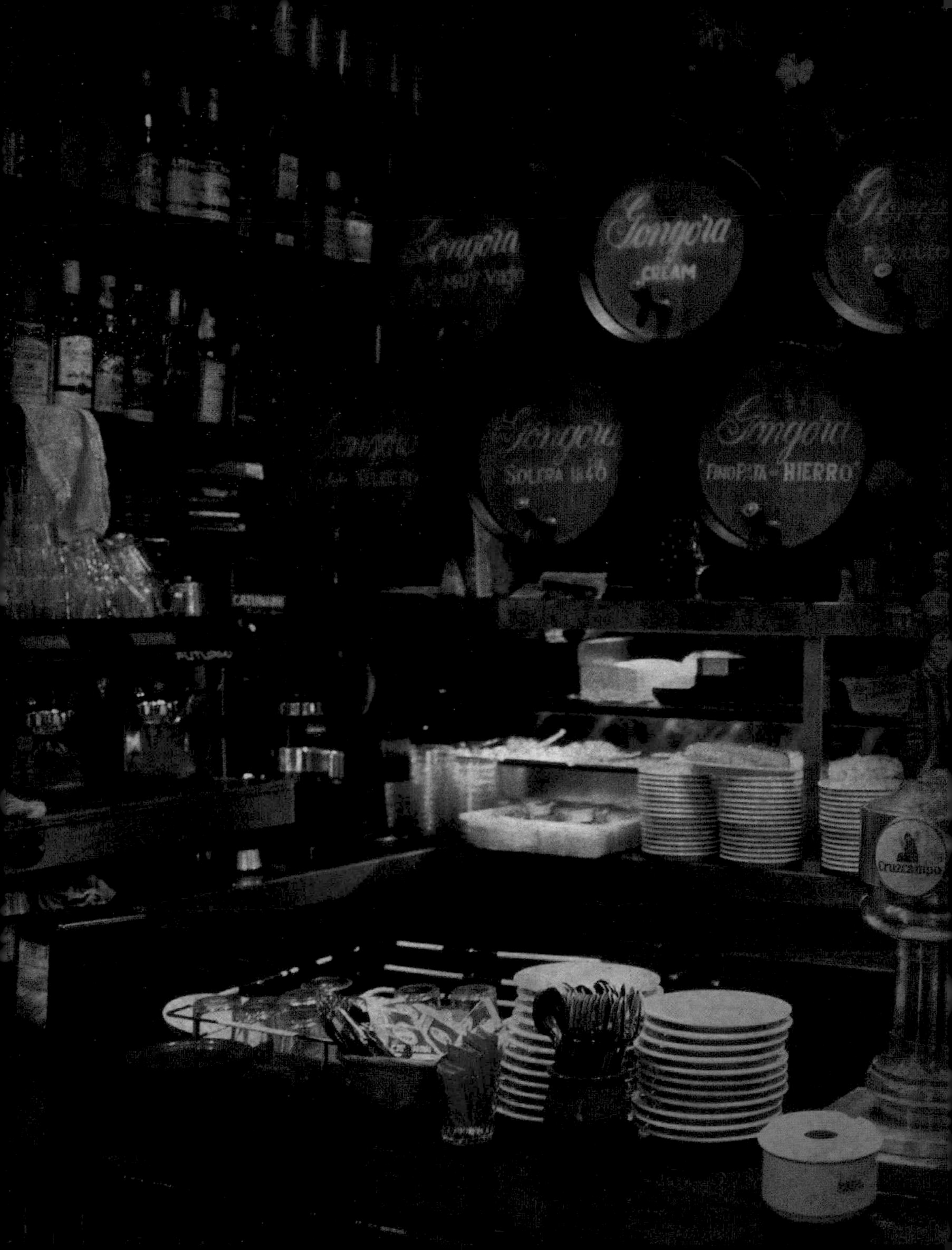
Gongora
CREAM
Gongora
Gongora
HIERRO
Cruzcampo

Carefully cut olives along the open cavity so they are opened out, but still in one piece.

Mash the goat's cheese, capers, garlic and parsley together in a small bowl, then season. Push an even amount of the mixture into the cavity of the olives, then press them closed.

Put flour in one small bowl, the egg in another and combine breadcrumbs and extra parsley in a third. Dip each olive into the flour, then into the egg and, finally, into the breadcrumbs. Put the crumbed olives on a plate. Refrigerate for 2 hours.

Fill a deep heavy-based saucepan one-third full of oil and heat to 180°C (350°F), or until a cube of bread dropped into the oil browns in 15 seconds. Cook the olives in batches for 1–2 minutes, or until golden brown all over; you may need to turn them with tongs or a long-handled metal spoon. Drain on crumpled paper towels and season. Serve warm or at room temperature with lemon wedges.

Note: If you can't find large pitted olives, buy stuffed ones and remove the filling.

White bean dip

2 x 400 g (14 oz) cans lima or cannellini beans, drained and rinsed

125 ml (4 fl oz/½ cup) olive oil

80 ml (2 ½ fl oz/⅓ cup) lemon juice

3 garlic cloves, finely chopped

1 tablespoon finely chopped fresh rosemary

Place the beans in a food processor with the oil, lemon juice, garlic and rosemary and 1 teaspoon salt. Process until smooth, then season with cracked black pepper.

Note: This dip improves with age, so you can make it up to 2 days ahead of time.

Cheese sticks

PREPARATION *25 minutes*
COOKING *10 minutes*   MAKES *30*

155 g (5½ oz/1¼ cups) plain
(all-purpose) flour

100 g (3¾ oz) unsalted
butter, chilled and chopped

100 g (3½ oz/¾ cup) grated
Gruyère cheese

1 tablespoon finely chopped
fresh oregano

1 egg yolk

1 tablespoon sea salt flakes

Line two baking trays with baking paper. Put flour and butter
in a food processor and process in short bursts until mixture
resembles fine breadcrumbs. Add Gruyère and oregano and
process for 10 seconds, or until just combined. Add egg yolk
and about 1 tablespoon water, and process until the dough just
comes together.

Turn the dough out onto a lightly floured surface and gather
into a ball. Form 2 teaspoons of dough into a ball, then roll
out into a stick about 12 cm (5 inch) long and place on the
baking trays. Repeat with the remaining dough, then cover
with plastic wrap and refrigerate for 15–20 minutes. Preheat
the oven to 200°C (400°F/Gas 6).

Lightly brush sticks with water and sprinkle with the sea salt
flakes. Bake for 10 minutes, or until golden. Cool on a wire
rack and serve with dips or as part of an antipasto platter.

Note: Cheese sticks will keep for up to 1 week when stored in
an airtight container.

Warm olives with lemon and herbs

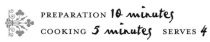

PREPARATION 10 minutes
COOKING 5 minutes SERVES 4

350 g (12 oz/2 cups) cured
  cracked green or black
  kalamata olives

80 ml (2½ fl oz/⅓ cup) olive
  oil

1 teaspoon fennel seeds

2 garlic cloves, finely
  chopped

pinch of cayenne pepper

finely shredded zest and juice
  of 1 lemon

1 tablespoon finely chopped
  coriander (cilantro) leaves

1 tablespoon finely chopped
  flat-leaf (Italian) parsley

Rinse the olives, drain and place in a saucepan with enough
water to cover.

Bring to the boil and cook for 5 minutes, then drain in a sieve.
Set aside. Add the olive oil and fennel seeds to the saucepan
and heat gently until fragrant.

Add the garlic, olives, cayenne pepper and the lemon zest and
juice. Toss for 2 minutes, or until the olives are hot.

Transfer to a bowl and toss with the coriander and parsley.
Serve hot with crusty bread to soak up the juices.

Garlic mushrooms

PREPARATION 10 minutes
COOKING 10 minutes SERVES 4

6 garlic cloves

1½ tablespoons lemon juice

655 g (1 lb 7 oz/7¼ cups) mushrooms (such as button, Swiss brown or pine), sliced

60 ml (2 fl oz/¼ cup) olive oil

½ small red chilli, seeded and finely chopped

2 teaspoons chopped flat-leaf (Italian) parsley

Crush four of the garlic cloves and thinly slice the rest. Sprinkle the lemon juice over the sliced mushrooms.

Heat oil in a large frying pan and add the crushed garlic and chopped chilli. Stir over medium–high heat for 10 seconds, then add the mushrooms. Season and then cook, stirring often, for 8–10 minutes or until the mushrooms are tender. Stir in the sliced garlic and the parsley and cook for another minute. Serve hot.

Sigara Boregi

PREPARATION **25 minutes** COOKING **10 minutes** MAKES **12**

500 g (1 lb 2 oz) English
  spinach

1 tablespoon olive oil

4 garlic cloves, crushed

200 g (7 oz) French shallots,
  finely chopped

75 g (2½ oz/½ cup) crumbled
  feta cheese

1 egg, lightly beaten

3 tablespoons chopped fresh
  flat-leaf (Italian) parsley

¼ teaspoon finely grated
  lemon zest

¼ teaspoon paprika

pinch of nutmeg

6 sheets filo pastry

125 g butter, melted

olive oil, for deep-frying

The little TAPAS book

Wash spinach, leaving it quite wet. Place in a saucepan, cover and cook over low heat until just wilted. Tip the spinach into a colander and press out the liquid with a wooden spoon. When cool, squeeze dry.

Heat the oil in a frying pan, and cook garlic and shallots for 2 minutes, or until soft but not browned. Transfer to a bowl and add the feta cheese, the egg, parsley, spinach and lemon zest. Season with paprika, nutmeg and salt and pepper, and mix well.

Brush a sheet of filo with melted butter, then fold it in half lengthways. It should measure 33 x 12 cm (13 x 4½ inch). Cut in half widthways. Brush with the butter, place 1 heaped tablespoon of filling at one end of each piece and spread to within 1 cm (½ inch) of each side. Fold in sides to cover edges of filling, continuing folds right up the length of the pastry. Brush with melted butter, then roll up tightly. Brush outside with butter and seal. Cover with a damp tea towel while you prepare the rest.

Heat the light olive oil in a deep frying pan to 180°C (350°F), or until a cube of bread browns in 15 seconds. Deep-fry in batches until golden. Serve warm or at room temperature.

SIDRERIA
CASA PARRONDO

SIDRA DE LA CASA	5
CERVEZA DE BARRIL	2
CAÑA DE CERVEZA	1,50
VINO DE RIOJA CRIANZA	2,5
VINO DE ALVARIÑO	2
VINO DE LA CASA	1,50
LICORES DE LA CASA	3,50
ZUMOS NATURALES	3,50
REFRESCOS	2
WHISKY NACIONAL	4
WHISKY DE IMPORTACIÓN	7
COMBINADOS	4
COMBINADOS RESERVA	7
VINOS FINOS	3
CAFE O INFUSION	1,50
VASO DE LECHE	1
SIDRA DULCE	7
COPA DE SIDRA	2
	9
	30

Potato, goat's cheese and herb tortilla

PREPARATION **15 minutes**
COOKING **30 minutes** MAKES **8-10 pieces**

1 tablespoon olive oil

2 small potatoes (all-purpose), peeled and diced

1 small red onion, finely chopped

75 g (2½ oz/½ cup) goat's cheese, crumbled

6 eggs

1 tablespoon chopped parsley

½ teaspoon thyme leaves

Heat the oil in a 19 cm (7½ inch) ovenproof frying pan over low—medium heat and cook potatoes for 10 minutes, turning often. Add the onion and continue to cook, turning often, for a further 10 minutes. Remove from the heat and sprinkle on the goat's cheese.

Preheat the grill (broiler) to medium. Combine the eggs in a bowl with the parsley and thyme and season well. Return the frying pan to medium heat and gently pour egg mixture over potatoes. Cook for 3–4 minutes, or until sides begin to puff up (gently lift the tortilla with a spatula occasionally to check that it is not burning).

Cook under the grill for 4–5 minutes, or until set on top. Cool, then slide onto a chopping board and cut into small wedges. Serve warm.

Herbed goat's cheese

PREPARATION *20 minutes*
COOKING *10 minutes* SERVES *6-8*

200 g (7 oz) vine leaves in brine

3 teaspoons green or pink peppercorns, drained and chopped

1 tablespoon chopped marjoram

3 x 100 g (3½ oz) rounds soft goat's cheese

Place the vine leaves in a heatproof bowl and cover with hot water to rinse away the brine. Drain well and pat dry with paper towels.

Combine peppercorns and marjoram in a shallow bowl. Toss the goat's cheese in the mixture until the sides are well coated.

Arrange a few vine leaves, shiny side down, on a work surface. Wrap each goat's cheese round in a few layers of vine leaves.

Cook the cheese on a barbecue hotplate or under a hot grill (broiler) for 3 minutes each side, or until the outside leaves are charred. Transfer to a plate and then allow to cool to room temperature. (The cheese is too soft to serve when hot, but will firm as it cools.) Use scissors to cut away vine leaves and serve the cheese with the rye bread.

Note: If desired, the cheese can be wrapped in vine leaves a few hours ahead.

Index

A
allioli 111
arancini 20
artichokes
  Russian salad 69
  warm dip 137

B
beans
  broad bean
    dip 116–17
  broad beans with
    jamón 41
  white bean dip 172
beef quesadillas, chilli 19
bondas 166–7
breadcrumbs, fried,
  with eggs 11
broad bean dip 116–17
broad beans with
  jamón 41

C
calamari
  fried 100
  pan-fried 56
capsicums
  marinated 125
  roasted 126
cheese
  cheese fritters 147
  cheese sticks 175
  chilli beef quesadillas
    19
  herbed goat's cheese
    187
  little sandwiches 47
  olive basil cheese
    spread 153
  potato, goat's cheese
    and herb tortilla 184

spinach and feta
  triangles 139
stuffed chillies 157
tomato and haloumi
  skewers 162
zucchini and haloumi
  fritters 154
chickpeas, fried 119
chilli
  chilli beef quesadillas
    19
  chilli olives 134
  polenta chillies 129
  stuffed chillies 157
chorizo
  chorizo in cider 7
  chorizo and tomato
    salsa 28
  fried breadcrumbs
    with eggs 11
  cider, chorizo in 7
concassé 112
Cordoban pork rolls 31
croquettes 34

D
dips
  broad bean 116–17
  warm artichoke 137
  white bean 172

E
eggs
  fried breadcrumbs
    with eggs 11
  potato, goat's cheese
    and herb tortilla 184
  tortilla 108
empanadas, tuna 76
empanadillas, ham
  and olive 8

F
fish and cumin
  kebabs 65
focaccia, mini, with
  roasted vegetables 161
fritters
  cheese 147
  prawn 55
  salt cod 96
  scallop 82
whitebait, with tartare
  sauce 59
zucchini and haloumi
  154

G
garlic
  fried potatoes with
    garlic mayonnaise 111
  garlic lamb skewers 15
  garlic mushrooms 179
  garlic prawns 66
goat's cheese, herbed 187
grissini wrapped in
  smoked salmon 95

H
ham
  broad beans with
    jamón 41
  croquettes 34
  ham and olive
    empanadillas 8
  little sandwiches 47
  mushroom and
    prosciutto skewers 39
  herbed goat's cheese 187

K
kibbeh 25

L
lamb
  garlic lamb skewers
    15
  kibbeh 25
  lamb and filo cigars 42

M
mayonnaise 69
meat sauce 20
meatballs 16–17
mushrooms
  croquettes 34
  garlic mushrooms 179
  mushroom and
    prosciutto skewers 39
  mushrooms with two
    sauces 142
mussels, stuffed 72

N
nuts, sweet and salty 130

O
olives
  chilli olives 134
  ham and olive
    empanadillas 8
  olive basil cheese
    spread 153
  olive tapenade 91
  stuffed black olives
    168
  tuna skewers 62
  warm olives with
    lemon and herbs 176
oysters and lemon herb
  dressing 88

Index

p

pastries
  fried pastries with
    seafood 51
  ham and olive
    empanadillas 8
  lamb and filo cigars 42
  sigara Boregi 180
  spinach and feta
    triangles 139
  tuna empanadas 76
peppers *see* capsicums
picada 56
pizza, Spanish 120
polenta chillies 129
pork, Cordoban rolls 31
potatoes
  bondas 166–7
  fried potato cakes 133
  fried potatoes with
    garlic mayonnaise 111
  potato, goat's cheese
    and herb tortilla 184
  potatoes in spicy
    tomato sauce 148
  tortilla 108
prawns
  garlic prawns 66
  grilled prawns with
    tequila mayonnaise 81
  prawn fritters 55
  prawns with romesco
    sauce 103

Q

quesadillas, chilli beef 19

R

rice, arancini 20
romesco sauce 103
Russian salad 69

s

saffron fish balls in
  tomato sauce 85
salad, Russian 69
salmon, smoked, grissini
  wrapped in 95
salsa, chorizo and tomato
  28
salt cod fritters 96
salt and pepper squid
  92–3
sandwiches, little 47
sauces
  mayonnaise 69
  meat sauce 20
  romesco 103
  spicy tomato 16
  tartare sauce 59
  tomato sauce 85
  white sauce 72
scallop fritters 82
seafood
  fish and cumin kebabs
    65
  fried calamari 100
  fried pastries with
    seafood 51
  garlic prawns 66
  grilled prawns with
    tequila mayonnaise 81
  grissini wrapped in
    smoked salmon 95
  oysters and lemon
    herb dressing 88
  pan-fried calamari 56
  prawn fritters 55
  prawns with romesco
    sauce 103
  saffron fish balls in
    tomato sauce 85
  salt cod fritters 96
  salt and pepper squid
    92–3

scallop fritters 82
stuffed mussels 72
tuna empanadas 76
tuna skewers 62
whitebait fritters with
  tartare sauce 59
sigara Boregi 180
skewers
  chargrilled vegetable
    112
  fish and cumin kebabs
    65
  garlic lamb skewers 15
  mushroom and
    prosciutto 39
  tomato and haloumi
    162
  tuna skewers 62
Spanish pizza 120
spinach
  sigara Boregi 180
  Spanish pizza 120
  spinach and feta
    triangles 139
squid, salt and
  pepper 92–3
sweet and salty nuts 130

t

tapenade, olive 91
tartare sauce 59
toast with tomato 165
tomatoes
  chorizo and tomato
    salsa 28
  concassé 112
  meatballs 16–17
  potatoes in spicy
    tomato sauce 148
  saffron fish balls in
    tomato sauce 85
  Spanish pizza 120

toast with tomato 165
tomato and haloumi
  skewers 162
tortilla 108
  potato, goat's cheese
    and herb 184
tuna empanadas 76
tuna skewers 62

v

vegetables
  broad bean dip 116–17
  chargrilled vegetable
    skewers 112
  fried chickpeas 119
  fried potato cakes 133
  fried potatoes with
    garlic mayonnaise 111
  marinated capsicums
    125
  mini focaccia with
    roasted vegetables
    161
  mushrooms with two
    sauces 142
  roasted capsicums 126
  warm artichoke dip 137

w

white bean dip 172
white sauce 72
whitebait fritters with
  tartare sauce 59

z

zucchini and haloumi
  fritters 154